This Book Belongs To:

____

____

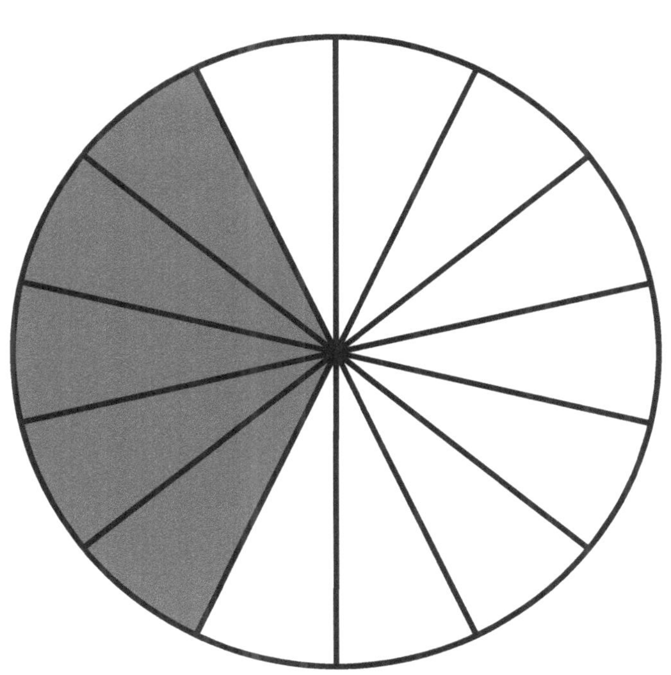

Fractions of Whole Numbers

1) $\frac{1}{3}$ of 12 = _______   2) $\frac{1}{2}$ of 10 = _______   3) $\frac{1}{3}$ of 15 = _______

4) $\frac{1}{3}$ of 0 = _______   5) $\frac{1}{2}$ of 8 = _______   6) $\frac{1}{4}$ of 12 = _______

7) $\frac{1}{3}$ of 6 = _______   8) $\frac{1}{4}$ of 20 = _______   9) $\frac{1}{3}$ of 12 = _______

10) $\frac{1}{3}$ of 9 = _______   11) $\frac{1}{3}$ of 6 = _______   12) $\frac{1}{4}$ of 16 = _______

13) $\frac{1}{2}$ of 4 = _______   14) $\frac{1}{3}$ of 12 = _______   15) $\frac{1}{2}$ of 8 = _______

16) $\frac{1}{2}$ of 10 = _______   17) $\frac{1}{2}$ of 8 = _______   18) $\frac{1}{3}$ of 12 = _______

19) $\frac{1}{2}$ of 6 = _______   20) $\frac{1}{3}$ of 12 = _______   21) $\frac{1}{3}$ of 12 = _______

22) $\frac{1}{4}$ of 12 = _______   23) $\frac{1}{3}$ of 15 = _______   24) $\frac{1}{3}$ of 15 = _______

25) $\frac{1}{3}$ of 6 = _______   26) $\frac{1}{4}$ of 16 = _______   27) $\frac{1}{2}$ of 4 = _______

28) $\frac{1}{2}$ of 0 = _______   29) $\frac{1}{3}$ of 3 = _______   30) $\frac{1}{2}$ of 2 = _______

1) $\frac{1}{3}$ of 12 = _______

2) $\frac{1}{4}$ of 4 = _______

3) $\frac{1}{3}$ of 3 = _______

4) $\frac{1}{2}$ of 8 = _______

5) $\frac{1}{3}$ of 9 = _______

6) $\frac{1}{4}$ of 8 = _______

7) $\frac{1}{4}$ of 8 = _______

8) $\frac{1}{3}$ of 9 = _______

9) $\frac{1}{2}$ of 8 = _______

10) $\frac{1}{3}$ of 3 = _______

11) $\frac{1}{3}$ of 6 = _______

12) $\frac{1}{3}$ of 9 = _______

13) $\frac{1}{2}$ of 4 = _______

14) $\frac{1}{3}$ of 6 = _______

15) $\frac{1}{3}$ of 6 = _______

16) $\frac{1}{4}$ of 16 = _______

17) $\frac{1}{2}$ of 2 = _______

18) $\frac{1}{2}$ of 6 = _______

19) $\frac{1}{2}$ of 8 = _______

20) $\frac{1}{4}$ of 8 = _______

21) $\frac{1}{3}$ of 15 = _______

22) $\frac{1}{4}$ of 12 = _______

23) $\frac{1}{3}$ of 12 = _______

24) $\frac{1}{3}$ of 6 = _______

25) $\frac{1}{3}$ of 15 = _______

26) $\frac{1}{4}$ of 12 = _______

27) $\frac{1}{4}$ of 20 = _______

28) $\frac{1}{3}$ of 9 = _______

29) $\frac{1}{3}$ of 3 = _______

30) $\frac{1}{4}$ of 12 = _______

1) $\frac{1}{3}$ of 12 = _______

2) $\frac{1}{3}$ of 3 = _______

3) $\frac{1}{4}$ of 4 = _______

4) $\frac{1}{3}$ of 9 = _______

5) $\frac{1}{4}$ of 12 = _______

6) $\frac{1}{2}$ of 10 = _______

7) $\frac{1}{3}$ of 15 = _______

8) $\frac{1}{2}$ of 6 = _______

9) $\frac{1}{2}$ of 10 = _______

10) $\frac{1}{4}$ of 12 = _______

11) $\frac{1}{2}$ of 2 = _______

12) $\frac{1}{4}$ of 0 = _______

13) $\frac{1}{3}$ of 12 = _______

14) $\frac{1}{2}$ of 2 = _______

15) $\frac{1}{4}$ of 4 = _______

16) $\frac{1}{2}$ of 8 = _______

17) $\frac{1}{2}$ of 8 = _______

18) $\frac{1}{3}$ of 3 = _______

19) $\frac{1}{2}$ of 8 = _______

20) $\frac{1}{4}$ of 16 = _______

21) $\frac{1}{4}$ of 16 = _______

22) $\frac{1}{4}$ of 8 = _______

23) $\frac{1}{4}$ of 12 = _______

24) $\frac{1}{2}$ of 8 = _______

25) $\frac{1}{4}$ of 20 = _______

26) $\frac{1}{3}$ of 12 = _______

27) $\frac{1}{3}$ of 12 = _______

28) $\frac{1}{3}$ of 6 = _______

29) $\frac{1}{4}$ of 12 = _______

30) $\frac{1}{4}$ of 20 = _______

$\frac{1}{3}$

1) $\frac{1}{4}$ of 12 = _______

2) $\frac{1}{4}$ of 20 = _______

3) $\frac{1}{2}$ of 8 = _______

4) $\frac{1}{2}$ of 10 = _______

5) $\frac{1}{2}$ of 10 = _______

6) $\frac{1}{2}$ of 2 = _______

7) $\frac{1}{3}$ of 3 = _______

8) $\frac{1}{2}$ of 10 = _______

9) $\frac{1}{2}$ of 8 = _______

10) $\frac{1}{4}$ of 12 = _______

11) $\frac{1}{3}$ of 6 = _______

12) $\frac{1}{4}$ of 12 = _______

13) $\frac{1}{4}$ of 12 = _______

14) $\frac{1}{2}$ of 10 = _______

15) $\frac{1}{2}$ of 4 = _______

16) $\frac{1}{2}$ of 4 = _______

17) $\frac{1}{2}$ of 10 = _______

18) $\frac{1}{3}$ of 15 = _______

19) $\frac{1}{2}$ of 10 = _______

20) $\frac{1}{3}$ of 15 = _______

21) $\frac{1}{4}$ of 4 = _______

22) $\frac{1}{3}$ of 6 = _______

23) $\frac{1}{4}$ of 20 = _______

24) $\frac{1}{2}$ of 10 = _______

25) $\frac{1}{2}$ of 6 = _______

26) $\frac{1}{4}$ of 4 = _______

27) $\frac{1}{3}$ of 3 = _______

28) $\frac{1}{2}$ of 10 = _______

29) $\frac{1}{3}$ of 0 = _______

30) $\frac{1}{4}$ of 4 = _______

1) $\frac{1}{2}$ of 10 = _______

2) $\frac{1}{2}$ of 2 = _______

3) $\frac{1}{4}$ of 16 = _______

4) $\frac{1}{4}$ of 4 = _______

5) $\frac{1}{2}$ of 4 = _______

6) $\frac{1}{2}$ of 4 = _______

7) $\frac{1}{4}$ of 20 = _______

8) $\frac{1}{2}$ of 6 = _______

9) $\frac{1}{4}$ of 16 = _______

10) $\frac{1}{4}$ of 4 = _______

11) $\frac{1}{2}$ of 4 = _______

12) $\frac{1}{2}$ of 4 = _______

13) $\frac{1}{3}$ of 6 = _______

14) $\frac{1}{2}$ of 4 = _______

15) $\frac{1}{3}$ of 9 = _______

16) $\frac{1}{2}$ of 4 = _______

17) $\frac{1}{3}$ of 9 = _______

18) $\frac{1}{2}$ of 6 = _______

19) $\frac{1}{3}$ of 3 = _______

20) $\frac{1}{4}$ of 4 = _______

21) $\frac{1}{2}$ of 8 = _______

22) $\frac{1}{4}$ of 20 = _______

23) $\frac{1}{2}$ of 2 = _______

24) $\frac{1}{4}$ of 20 = _______

25) $\frac{1}{4}$ of 8 = _______

26) $\frac{1}{4}$ of 12 = _______

27) $\frac{1}{3}$ of 12 = _______

28) $\frac{1}{3}$ of 9 = _______

29) $\frac{1}{4}$ of 12 = _______

30) $\frac{1}{3}$ of 15 = _______

1) $\frac{1}{3}$ of 3 = _______

2) $\frac{1}{2}$ of 8 = _______

3) $\frac{1}{3}$ of 15 = _______

4) $\frac{1}{3}$ of 6 = _______

5) $\frac{1}{2}$ of 8 = _______

6) $\frac{1}{4}$ of 16 = _______

7) $\frac{1}{4}$ of 12 = _______

8) $\frac{1}{3}$ of 15 = _______

9) $\frac{1}{3}$ of 15 = _______

10) $\frac{1}{2}$ of 8 = _______

11) $\frac{1}{4}$ of 4 = _______

12) $\frac{1}{4}$ of 20 = _______

13) $\frac{1}{3}$ of 9 = _______

14) $\frac{1}{4}$ of 4 = _______

15) $\frac{1}{4}$ of 4 = _______

16) $\frac{1}{3}$ of 9 = _______

17) $\frac{1}{3}$ of 9 = _______

18) $\frac{1}{3}$ of 12 = _______

19) $\frac{1}{4}$ of 4 = _______

20) $\frac{1}{3}$ of 15 = _______

21) $\frac{1}{2}$ of 4 = _______

22) $\frac{1}{2}$ of 8 = _______

23) $\frac{1}{4}$ of 8 = _______

24) $\frac{1}{4}$ of 8 = _______

25) $\frac{1}{2}$ of 6 = _______

26) $\frac{1}{3}$ of 12 = _______

27) $\frac{1}{3}$ of 9 = _______

28) $\frac{1}{3}$ of 9 = _______

29) $\frac{1}{3}$ of 0 = _______

30) $\frac{1}{4}$ of 4 = _______

1) $\frac{1}{3}$ of 9 = _______

2) $\frac{1}{4}$ of 4 = _______

3) $\frac{1}{3}$ of 15 = _______

4) $\frac{1}{3}$ of 3 = _______

5) $\frac{1}{3}$ of 3 = _______

6) $\frac{1}{2}$ of 10 = _______

7) $\frac{1}{4}$ of 16 = _______

8) $\frac{1}{4}$ of 8 = _______

9) $\frac{1}{4}$ of 16 = _______

10) $\frac{1}{3}$ of 6 = _______

11) $\frac{1}{4}$ of 4 = _______

12) $\frac{1}{2}$ of 10 = _______

13) $\frac{1}{3}$ of 3 = _______

14) $\frac{1}{4}$ of 8 = _______

15) $\frac{1}{4}$ of 20 = _______

16) $\frac{1}{3}$ of 12 = _______

17) $\frac{1}{3}$ of 12 = _______

18) $\frac{1}{4}$ of 20 = _______

19) $\frac{1}{2}$ of 4 = _______

20) $\frac{1}{2}$ of 6 = _______

21) $\frac{1}{2}$ of 2 = _______

22) $\frac{1}{2}$ of 8 = _______

23) $\frac{1}{2}$ of 4 = _______

24) $\frac{1}{4}$ of 16 = _______

25) $\frac{1}{3}$ of 12 = _______

26) $\frac{1}{3}$ of 12 = _______

27) $\frac{1}{2}$ of 6 = _______

28) $\frac{1}{2}$ of 8 = _______

29) $\frac{1}{2}$ of 10 = _______

30) $\frac{1}{2}$ of 8 = _______

1) $\frac{1}{2}$ of 6 = _______

2) $\frac{1}{3}$ of 9 = _______

3) $\frac{1}{2}$ of 2 = _______

4) $\frac{1}{4}$ of 4 = _______

5) $\frac{1}{4}$ of 16 = _______

6) $\frac{1}{4}$ of 12 = _______

7) $\frac{1}{4}$ of 8 = _______

8) $\frac{1}{4}$ of 12 = _______

9) $\frac{1}{4}$ of 16 = _______

10) $\frac{1}{4}$ of 8 = _______

11) $\frac{1}{2}$ of 4 = _______

12) $\frac{1}{2}$ of 10 = _______

13) $\frac{1}{4}$ of 4 = _______

14) $\frac{1}{3}$ of 6 = _______

15) $\frac{1}{3}$ of 3 = _______

16) $\frac{1}{2}$ of 8 = _______

17) $\frac{1}{3}$ of 15 = _______

18) $\frac{1}{2}$ of 4 = _______

19) $\frac{1}{3}$ of 9 = _______

20) $\frac{1}{3}$ of 9 = _______

21) $\frac{1}{3}$ of 3 = _______

22) $\frac{1}{3}$ of 12 = _______

23) $\frac{1}{4}$ of 4 = _______

24) $\frac{1}{2}$ of 4 = _______

25) $\frac{1}{3}$ of 15 = _______

26) $\frac{1}{3}$ of 3 = _______

27) $\frac{1}{4}$ of 8 = _______

28) $\frac{1}{3}$ of 9 = _______

29) $\frac{1}{2}$ of 4 = _______

30) $\frac{1}{3}$ of 6 = _______

1) $\frac{1}{3}$ of 15 = _______

2) $\frac{1}{4}$ of 8 = _______

3) $\frac{1}{4}$ of 16 = _______

4) $\frac{1}{4}$ of 12 = _______

5) $\frac{1}{3}$ of 12 = _______

6) $\frac{1}{4}$ of 4 = _______

7) $\frac{1}{2}$ of 8 = _______

8) $\frac{1}{2}$ of 2 = _______

9) $\frac{1}{3}$ of 12 = _______

10) $\frac{1}{4}$ of 16 = _______

11) $\frac{1}{2}$ of 8 = _______

12) $\frac{1}{2}$ of 6 = _______

13) $\frac{1}{2}$ of 10 = _______

14) $\frac{1}{3}$ of 9 = _______

15) $\frac{1}{2}$ of 10 = _______

16) $\frac{1}{4}$ of 16 = _______

17) $\frac{1}{2}$ of 2 = _______

18) $\frac{1}{4}$ of 0 = _______

19) $\frac{1}{2}$ of 2 = _______

20) $\frac{1}{3}$ of 12 = _______

21) $\frac{1}{2}$ of 10 = _______

22) $\frac{1}{2}$ of 4 = _______

23) $\frac{1}{2}$ of 4 = _______

24) $\frac{1}{4}$ of 4 = _______

25) $\frac{1}{3}$ of 12 = _______

26) $\frac{1}{4}$ of 16 = _______

27) $\frac{1}{4}$ of 12 = _______

28) $\frac{1}{3}$ of 6 = _______

29) $\frac{1}{3}$ of 6 = _______

30) $\frac{1}{3}$ of 9 = _______

1) $\frac{1}{3}$ of 6 = ______

2) $\frac{1}{2}$ of 4 = ______

3) $\frac{1}{4}$ of 4 = ______

4) $\frac{1}{3}$ of 15 = ______

5) $\frac{1}{3}$ of 3 = ______

6) $\frac{1}{2}$ of 8 = ______

7) $\frac{1}{4}$ of 12 = ______

8) $\frac{1}{4}$ of 16 = ______

9) $\frac{1}{2}$ of 8 = ______

10) $\frac{1}{4}$ of 8 = ______

11) $\frac{1}{2}$ of 10 = ______

12) $\frac{1}{3}$ of 12 = ______

13) $\frac{1}{3}$ of 6 = ______

14) $\frac{1}{3}$ of 12 = ______

15) $\frac{1}{3}$ of 12 = ______

16) $\frac{1}{2}$ of 4 = ______

17) $\frac{1}{2}$ of 10 = ______

18) $\frac{1}{3}$ of 3 = ______

19) $\frac{1}{4}$ of 16 = ______

20) $\frac{1}{4}$ of 20 = ______

21) $\frac{1}{3}$ of 9 = ______

22) $\frac{1}{4}$ of 20 = ______

23) $\frac{1}{3}$ of 0 = ______

24) $\frac{1}{2}$ of 8 = ______

25) $\frac{1}{4}$ of 16 = ______

26) $\frac{1}{2}$ of 6 = ______

27) $\frac{1}{3}$ of 3 = ______

28) $\frac{1}{2}$ of 8 = ______

29) $\frac{1}{4}$ of 16 = ______

30) $\frac{1}{2}$ of 4 = ______

Adding Fractions

1) $\frac{1}{2} + \frac{1}{2} =$ 2) $\frac{1}{3} + \frac{3}{4} =$

3) $\frac{4}{5} + \frac{1}{2} =$ 4) $\frac{1}{4} + \frac{1}{2} =$

5) $\frac{1}{4} + \frac{2}{3} =$ 6) $\frac{1}{2} + \frac{2}{5} =$

7) $\frac{2}{3} + \frac{1}{3} =$ 8) $\frac{1}{2} + \frac{1}{3} =$

9) $\frac{2}{3} + \frac{3}{5} =$ 10) $\frac{3}{4} + \frac{1}{5} =$

11) $\frac{2}{3} + \frac{1}{5} =$ 12) $\frac{1}{3} + \frac{1}{2} =$

13) $\frac{4}{5} + \frac{1}{5} =$ 14) $\frac{1}{5} + \frac{2}{3} =$

11/42

15) $\frac{1}{2} + \frac{4}{5} =$ 16) $\frac{3}{4} + \frac{1}{3} =$

17) $\frac{2}{5} + \frac{2}{3} =$ 18) $\frac{1}{2} + \frac{1}{2} =$

19) $\frac{1}{2} + \frac{2}{3} =$ 20) $\frac{1}{3} + \frac{1}{2} =$

21) $\frac{1}{2} + \frac{2}{3} =$ 22) $\frac{1}{3} + \frac{1}{2} =$

23) $\frac{1}{2} + \frac{1}{2} =$ 24) $\frac{1}{5} + 1 =$

$\frac{1}{3}$

25) $\frac{2}{3} + \frac{3}{4} =$ 26) $\frac{1}{2} + \frac{1}{4} =$

27) $\frac{2}{3} + \frac{3}{5} =$ 28) $\frac{1}{3} + \frac{1}{2} =$

29) $\frac{1}{5} + 1 =$ 30) $\frac{1}{3} + \frac{1}{2} =$

1) $\frac{3}{5} + \frac{1}{2} =$ 2) $\frac{1}{2} + \frac{2}{5} =$

3) $\frac{3}{5} + \frac{4}{5} =$ 4) $\frac{1}{4} + \frac{3}{5} =$

5) $\frac{1}{3} + \frac{1}{2} =$ 6) $\frac{4}{5} + \frac{2}{3} =$

7) $\frac{1}{4} + \frac{2}{3} =$ 8) $\frac{3}{5} + \frac{1}{2} =$

9) $\frac{1}{3} + \frac{1}{4} =$ 10) $\frac{3}{4} + \frac{1}{5} =$

11) $\frac{3}{4} + \frac{2}{5} =$ 12) $\frac{1}{4} + \frac{3}{5} =$

13) $\frac{1}{3} + \frac{2}{5} =$ 14) $\frac{1}{4} + \frac{2}{3} =$

15) $\frac{2}{3} + \frac{1}{2} =$ 16) $\frac{1}{2} + \frac{1}{2} =$

17) $\frac{2}{3} + \frac{1}{2} =$ 18) $\frac{1}{2} + \frac{1}{4} =$

19) $\frac{1}{3} + \frac{4}{5} =$ 20) $\frac{2}{3} + \frac{1}{2} =$

21) $\frac{1}{2} + \frac{1}{3} =$ 22) $\frac{1}{3} + \frac{1}{3} =$

23) $\frac{3}{4} + \frac{1}{2} =$ 24) $\frac{2}{3} + \frac{1}{3} =$

25) $\frac{1}{2} + \frac{2}{3} =$ 26) $\frac{3}{4} + \frac{3}{4} =$

27) $\frac{1}{2} + \frac{1}{2} =$ 28) $\frac{2}{3} + \frac{1}{3} =$

29) $\frac{1}{3} + \frac{2}{5} =$ 30) $\frac{1}{2} + \frac{3}{4} =$

1) $\frac{3}{5} + \frac{1}{3} =$

2) $\frac{3}{4} + \frac{2}{5} =$

3) $\frac{3}{5} + \frac{1}{3} =$

4) $\frac{1}{2} + \frac{1}{5} =$

5) $\frac{1}{3} + \frac{1}{2} =$

6) $\frac{1}{2} + \frac{1}{4} =$

7) $\frac{2}{3} + \frac{4}{5} =$

8) $\frac{3}{4} + \frac{1}{2} =$

9) $\frac{3}{4} + \frac{3}{4} =$

10) $\frac{1}{2} + \frac{1}{2} =$

11) $\frac{1}{4} + \frac{1}{2} =$

12) $\frac{2}{5} + \frac{1}{2} =$

13) $\frac{1}{4} + \frac{2}{5} =$

14) $\frac{1}{2} + \frac{3}{4} =$

15) $\frac{3}{4} + \frac{1}{5} =$

16) $\frac{1}{3} + \frac{3}{4} =$

13/42

17) $\frac{1}{4} + \frac{1}{2} =$

18) $\frac{2}{3} + \frac{2}{3} =$

19) $\frac{1}{3} + \frac{4}{5} =$

20) $\frac{1}{2} + \frac{1}{2} =$

21) $\frac{3}{4} + \frac{1}{2} =$

22) $\frac{4}{5} + \frac{1}{2} =$

23) $\frac{2}{3} + \frac{2}{3} =$

24) $\frac{1}{2} + \frac{3}{4} =$

25) $\frac{1}{4} + \frac{1}{3} =$

26) $\frac{1}{2} + \frac{2}{5} =$

$\frac{1}{3}$

27) $\frac{2}{3} + \frac{1}{2} =$

28) $\frac{3}{5} + \frac{1}{2} =$

29) $\frac{2}{3} + \frac{1}{2} =$

30) $\frac{3}{5} + \frac{2}{3} =$

1) $\frac{3}{4} + \frac{2}{3} =$

2) $\frac{1}{2} + \frac{1}{2} =$

3) $\frac{1}{4} + \frac{1}{3} =$

4) $\frac{1}{5} + \frac{1}{3} =$

5) $\frac{1}{2} + \frac{3}{4} =$

6) $\frac{1}{2} + \frac{1}{3} =$

7) $\frac{1}{3} + \frac{1}{2} =$

8) $\frac{1}{3} + \frac{2}{3} =$

9) $\frac{3}{4} + \frac{3}{4} =$

10) $\frac{2}{5} + \frac{2}{3} =$

11) $\frac{2}{3} + \frac{3}{4} =$

12) $\frac{1}{2} + \frac{3}{5} =$

13) $\frac{1}{2} + \frac{1}{2} =$

14) $\frac{4}{5} + \frac{1}{3} =$

15) $\frac{1}{2} + \frac{2}{3} =$

16) $\frac{2}{3} + \frac{1}{2} =$

17) $\frac{1}{2} + \frac{1}{3} =$

18) $\frac{2}{5} + \frac{1}{5} =$

19) $\frac{1}{3} + \frac{1}{2} =$

20) $\frac{1}{3} + \frac{3}{5} =$

21) $\frac{1}{2} + \frac{1}{2} =$

22) $\frac{1}{3} + \frac{3}{4} =$

23) $\frac{1}{2} + \frac{1}{2} =$

24) $\frac{1}{4} + \frac{2}{3} =$

25) $\frac{1}{2} + \frac{1}{3} =$

26) $\frac{1}{2} + \frac{2}{3} =$

27) $\frac{4}{5} + \frac{1}{2} =$

28) $\frac{2}{5} + \frac{1}{2} =$

29) $\frac{4}{5} + \frac{2}{3} =$

30) $\frac{1}{2} + \frac{1}{4} =$

14/42

⅓

1) $\frac{1}{3} + \frac{1}{3} =$

2) $\frac{2}{5} + \frac{3}{4} =$

3) $\frac{2}{3} + \frac{3}{5} =$

4) $\frac{2}{3} + \frac{1}{2} =$

5) $\frac{2}{5} + \frac{1}{2} =$

6) $\frac{2}{3} + 1 =$

7) $\frac{1}{5} + \frac{1}{3} =$

8) $\frac{4}{5} + \frac{1}{2} =$

9) $\frac{2}{5} + \frac{3}{4} =$

10) $\frac{1}{2} + \frac{1}{2} =$

11) $\frac{1}{2} + \frac{3}{5} =$

12) $\frac{1}{4} + \frac{1}{4} =$

13) $\frac{1}{2} + \frac{1}{2} =$

14) $\frac{1}{2} + \frac{4}{5} =$

15) $\frac{1}{3} + \frac{1}{2} =$

16) $\frac{1}{2} + \frac{1}{4} =$

17) $\frac{1}{3} + \frac{1}{3} =$

18) $\frac{4}{5} + \frac{3}{4} =$

19) $\frac{1}{2} + \frac{1}{2} =$

20) $\frac{2}{3} + \frac{3}{4} =$

21) $\frac{1}{3} + \frac{4}{5} =$

22) $\frac{1}{2} + \frac{2}{3} =$

23) $\frac{1}{2} + \frac{1}{3} =$

24) $\frac{2}{3} + \frac{2}{3} =$

25) $\frac{3}{4} + \frac{2}{5} =$

26) $1 + \frac{3}{5} =$

27) $\frac{1}{2} + \frac{1}{5} =$

28) $\frac{2}{5} + \frac{1}{2} =$

29) $\frac{1}{2} + \frac{4}{5} =$

30) $\frac{4}{5} + \frac{1}{2} =$

15/42

$\frac{1}{3}$

1) $\frac{7}{2} + \frac{33}{8} =$

2) $\frac{19}{8} + \frac{7}{2} =$

3) $4 + \frac{7}{4} =$

4) $\frac{9}{2} + \frac{2}{5} =$

5) $\frac{15}{7} + \frac{5}{3} =$

6) $\frac{17}{5} + \frac{4}{5} =$

7) $\frac{39}{8} + \frac{19}{5} =$

8) $5 + \frac{19}{4} =$

9) $\frac{17}{5} + \frac{1}{2} =$

10) $3 + \frac{9}{8} =$

11) $\frac{9}{4} + \frac{9}{4} =$

12) $\frac{5}{2} + \frac{1}{3} =$

13) $\frac{5}{2} + \frac{7}{3} =$

14) $\frac{7}{5} + 3 =$

15) $\frac{11}{6} + \frac{31}{8} =$

16) $\frac{35}{8} + \frac{2}{3} =$

17) $\frac{9}{2} + \frac{17}{8} =$

18) $\frac{3}{7} + \frac{3}{2} =$

19) $\frac{4}{3} + \frac{10}{3} =$

20) $\frac{7}{3} + \frac{11}{5} =$

21) $3 + \frac{3}{7} =$

22) $\frac{12}{7} + \frac{6}{5} =$

23) $\frac{3}{8} + \frac{12}{7} =$

24) $1 + \frac{4}{3} =$

25) $4 + \frac{13}{4} =$

26) $\frac{29}{8} + \frac{9}{2} =$

27) $\frac{9}{8} + \frac{21}{5} =$

28) $\frac{17}{6} + 5 =$

29) $3 + \frac{15}{7} =$

30) $\frac{7}{3} + \frac{7}{2} =$

16/42

1) $\frac{1}{8} + \frac{31}{7} =$

2) $\frac{11}{3} + \frac{9}{2} =$

3) $\frac{10}{7} + 3 =$

4) $\frac{7}{2} + 4 =$

5) $\frac{1}{7} + 1 =$

6) $\frac{7}{3} + \frac{4}{3} =$

7) $\frac{23}{5} + \frac{13}{5} =$

8) $\frac{17}{4} + \frac{19}{4} =$

9) $\frac{5}{8} + \frac{7}{8} =$

10) $\frac{5}{2} + \frac{13}{5} =$

11) $5 + \frac{11}{8} =$

12) $\frac{19}{5} + \frac{7}{2} =$

13) $\frac{19}{6} + \frac{1}{3} =$

14) $\frac{12}{7} + \frac{20}{7} =$

15) $\frac{20}{7} + \frac{17}{8} =$

16) $\frac{19}{4} + 2 =$

17) $\frac{9}{2} + \frac{16}{3} =$

18) $\frac{17}{7} + \frac{11}{5} =$

19) $\frac{3}{5} + \frac{17}{4} =$

20) $\frac{4}{3} + \frac{8}{7} =$

21) $\frac{2}{3} + \frac{13}{4} =$

22) $\frac{7}{2} + \frac{22}{7} =$

23) $\frac{5}{2} + \frac{9}{2} =$

24) $\frac{29}{7} + 3 =$

25) $\frac{13}{4} + \frac{1}{6} =$

26) $\frac{4}{5} + \frac{14}{5} =$

27) $\frac{12}{5} + \frac{23}{7} =$

28) $\frac{2}{5} + \frac{3}{4} =$

29) $\frac{22}{7} + 3 =$

30) $\frac{23}{7} + \frac{30}{7} =$

17/42

⅓

1) $\frac{1}{6} + \frac{39}{8} =$

2) $\frac{14}{3} + \frac{5}{2} =$

3) $\frac{5}{8} + \frac{3}{5} =$

4) $5 + \frac{7}{2} =$

5) $\frac{5}{8} + 5 =$

6) $\frac{6}{5} + 4 =$

7) $\frac{8}{7} + \frac{15}{4} =$

8) $\frac{37}{8} + 5 =$

9) $3 + \frac{4}{3} =$

10) $4 + \frac{1}{3} =$

11) $\frac{1}{3} + \frac{5}{2} =$

12) $2 + \frac{13}{4} =$

13) $\frac{9}{4} + \frac{5}{7} =$

14) $1 + \frac{3}{4} =$

15) $\frac{34}{7} + \frac{21}{5} =$

16) $\frac{3}{2} + \frac{7}{2} =$

17) $\frac{31}{8} + \frac{11}{6} =$

18) $\frac{24}{5} + \frac{5}{2} =$

19) $\frac{9}{8} + \frac{3}{7} =$

20) $\frac{5}{2} + \frac{14}{3} =$

21) $\frac{7}{3} + 5 =$

22) $\frac{5}{3} + 3 =$

23) $2 + \frac{2}{3} =$

24) $\frac{1}{2} + 4 =$

25) $\frac{1}{3} + \frac{3}{2} =$

26) $4 + \frac{25}{7} =$

27) $4 + \frac{19}{4} =$

28) $\frac{7}{2} + \frac{15}{4} =$

29) $\frac{16}{7} + 3 =$

30) $\frac{4}{7} + \frac{24}{5} =$

1) $\frac{7}{2} + \frac{5}{4} =$

2) $5 + \frac{22}{5} =$

3) $\frac{5}{2} + \frac{6}{5} =$

4) $\frac{3}{2} + \frac{1}{2} =$

5) $\frac{35}{8} + \frac{3}{4} =$

6) $\frac{9}{4} + 5 =$

7) $3 + \frac{30}{7} =$

8) $4 + \frac{1}{2} =$

9) $\frac{1}{7} + 2 =$

10) $\frac{11}{5} + \frac{10}{3} =$

11) $\frac{16}{7} + \frac{9}{2} =$

12) $\frac{3}{2} + \frac{9}{2} =$

13) $5 + \frac{4}{5} =$

14) $\frac{25}{8} + \frac{23}{7} =$

15) $\frac{21}{8} + \frac{9}{2} =$

16) $5 + \frac{5}{6} =$

17) $\frac{3}{2} + \frac{3}{5} =$

18) $\frac{16}{5} + \frac{5}{3} =$

19) $\frac{16}{5} + 1 =$

20) $\frac{5}{3} + \frac{1}{2} =$

21) $\frac{32}{7} + 2 =$

22) $\frac{21}{5} + 3 =$

23) $\frac{3}{2} + \frac{19}{4} =$

24) $\frac{10}{3} + 3 =$

25) $\frac{9}{2} + 4 =$

26) $3 + \frac{9}{8} =$

27) $\frac{7}{2} + 1 =$

28) $5 + \frac{7}{2} =$

29) $\frac{15}{4} + \frac{1}{2} =$

30) $\frac{26}{7} + 2 =$

1) $\frac{17}{8} + 2 =$

2) $\frac{7}{2} + \frac{11}{8} =$

3) $\frac{3}{2} + \frac{7}{2} =$

4) $\frac{8}{3} + \frac{1}{3} =$

5) $5 + \frac{4}{3} =$

6) $\frac{23}{8} + \frac{3}{2} =$

7) $\frac{19}{4} + \frac{21}{5} =$

8) $\frac{5}{3} + \frac{5}{2} =$

9) $\frac{1}{8} + \frac{13}{5} =$

10) $5 + \frac{1}{2} =$

11) $\frac{22}{7} + \frac{6}{7} =$

12) $\frac{5}{4} + 2 =$

13) $\frac{2}{3} + \frac{7}{4} =$

14) $\frac{7}{3} + 4 =$

15) $\frac{7}{2} + \frac{9}{5} =$

16) $\frac{7}{2} + \frac{21}{5} =$

17) $\frac{5}{2} + 3 =$

18) $\frac{15}{7} + \frac{3}{2} =$

19) $\frac{29}{7} + \frac{29}{7} =$

20) $\frac{30}{7} + 5 =$

21) $\frac{4}{7} + 1 =$

22) $\frac{1}{6} + \frac{30}{7} =$

23) $\frac{33}{7} + \frac{9}{7} =$

24) $\frac{18}{5} + \frac{35}{8} =$

25) $\frac{9}{7} + \frac{8}{3} =$

26) $\frac{12}{5} + \frac{7}{3} =$

27) $\frac{5}{6} + \frac{1}{4} =$

28) $5 + \frac{15}{4} =$

29) $5 + \frac{11}{4} =$

30) $3 + \frac{19}{5} =$

Subtracting Fractions

1) $\frac{3}{4} - \frac{1}{2} =$

2) $\frac{2}{3} - \frac{1}{2} =$

3) $\frac{3}{5} - \frac{1}{2} =$

4) $\frac{3}{4} - \frac{1}{2} =$

5) $\frac{3}{5} - \frac{2}{5} =$

6) $\frac{1}{3} - \frac{1}{4} =$

7) $\frac{1}{2} - \frac{2}{5} =$

8) $\frac{3}{5} - \frac{1}{2} =$

9) $\frac{2}{5} - \frac{1}{3} =$

10) $\frac{1}{4} - \frac{1}{4} =$

11) $\frac{1}{2} - \frac{1}{5} =$

12) $\frac{1}{2} - \frac{2}{5} =$

13) $\frac{1}{2} - \frac{1}{2} =$

14) $\frac{3}{5} - \frac{1}{3} =$

15) $\frac{1}{2} - \frac{1}{4} =$

16) $\frac{2}{3} - \frac{1}{5} =$

17) $\frac{1}{2} - \frac{1}{2} =$

18) $\frac{1}{3} - \frac{1}{5} =$

19) $1 - \frac{3}{4} =$

20) $\frac{1}{2} - \frac{1}{4} =$

21) $\frac{3}{4} - \frac{1}{5} =$

22) $\frac{4}{5} - \frac{3}{4} =$

23) $1 - \frac{3}{5} =$

24) $\frac{1}{2} - \frac{1}{4} =$

25) $\frac{4}{5} - \frac{2}{3} =$

26) $\frac{1}{2} - \frac{1}{2} =$

27) $\frac{2}{3} - \frac{1}{3} =$

28) $\frac{3}{4} - \frac{1}{4} =$

29) $\frac{2}{3} - \frac{1}{3} =$

30) $\frac{1}{2} - \frac{1}{5} =$

1) $\frac{1}{2} - \frac{1}{3} =$

2) $1 - \frac{1}{2} =$

3) $\frac{3}{5} - \frac{1}{2} =$

4) $\frac{2}{3} - \frac{1}{2} =$

5) $\frac{4}{5} - \frac{1}{5} =$

6) $\frac{3}{4} - \frac{2}{5} =$

7) $\frac{1}{3} - \frac{1}{4} =$

8) $\frac{1}{2} - \frac{1}{5} =$

9) $\frac{4}{5} - \frac{1}{2} =$

10) $\frac{3}{4} - \frac{1}{2} =$

11) $\frac{4}{5} - \frac{1}{3} =$

12) $\frac{3}{4} - \frac{1}{3} =$

13) $\frac{1}{2} - \frac{1}{4} =$

14) $\frac{2}{3} - \frac{1}{2} =$

15) $\frac{1}{2} - \frac{1}{4} =$

16) $\frac{1}{4} - \frac{1}{5} =$

22/42

17) $\frac{4}{5} - \frac{1}{2} =$

18) $\frac{2}{3} - \frac{1}{5} =$

19) $\frac{1}{2} - \frac{1}{4} =$

20) $\frac{2}{5} - \frac{1}{4} =$

21) $\frac{4}{5} - \frac{1}{2} =$

22) $\frac{3}{5} - \frac{1}{2} =$

23) $\frac{2}{3} - \frac{1}{3} =$

24) $\frac{3}{5} - \frac{1}{4} =$

25) $\frac{4}{5} - \frac{1}{2} =$

1/3

26) $\frac{3}{5} - \frac{1}{5} =$

27) $\frac{3}{5} - \frac{2}{5} =$

28) $\frac{3}{4} - \frac{1}{2} =$

29) $1 - \frac{2}{5} =$

30) $\frac{1}{2} - \frac{1}{2} =$

1) $\frac{1}{4} - \frac{1}{4} =$

2) $\frac{1}{2} - \frac{1}{4} =$

3) $\frac{2}{3} - \frac{1}{2} =$

4) $\frac{1}{2} - \frac{1}{5} =$

5) $\frac{3}{4} - \frac{1}{2} =$

6) $\frac{2}{3} - \frac{1}{3} =$

7) $\frac{4}{5} - \frac{1}{2} =$

8) $\frac{1}{2} - \frac{1}{3} =$

9) $\frac{3}{4} - \frac{2}{3} =$

10) $\frac{1}{2} - \frac{1}{2} =$

11) $\frac{3}{4} - \frac{1}{3} =$

12) $1 - \frac{1}{4} =$

13) $\frac{1}{2} - \frac{1}{3} =$

14) $\frac{2}{5} - \frac{1}{3} =$

15) $\frac{4}{5} - \frac{1}{5} =$

16) $\frac{2}{3} - \frac{2}{5} =$

17) $\frac{2}{3} - \frac{1}{2} =$

18) $\frac{4}{5} - \frac{1}{2} =$

19) $\frac{3}{4} - \frac{1}{3} =$

20) $\frac{1}{2} - \frac{1}{3} =$

21) $\frac{3}{4} - \frac{1}{2} =$

22) $\frac{2}{3} - \frac{1}{3} =$

23) $\frac{1}{2} - \frac{2}{5} =$

24) $\frac{3}{4} - \frac{1}{2} =$

25) $\frac{2}{3} - \frac{1}{3} =$

26) $\frac{1}{2} - \frac{1}{4} =$

27) $\frac{2}{3} - \frac{1}{3} =$

28) $\frac{4}{5} - \frac{3}{5} =$

29) $\frac{1}{2} - \frac{2}{5} =$

30) $\frac{3}{4} - \frac{1}{2} =$

1) $\frac{3}{4} - \frac{2}{3} =$

2) $\frac{3}{4} - \frac{1}{2} =$

3) $\frac{4}{5} - \frac{1}{2} =$

4) $1 - \frac{3}{5} =$

5) $\frac{2}{3} - \frac{1}{2} =$

6) $\frac{3}{5} - \frac{1}{2} =$

7) $\frac{3}{4} - \frac{1}{5} =$

8) $\frac{1}{2} - \frac{1}{2} =$

9) $\frac{3}{4} - \frac{1}{2} =$

10) $\frac{4}{5} - \frac{2}{3} =$

11) $\frac{3}{5} - \frac{1}{2} =$

12) $\frac{1}{2} - \frac{1}{4} =$

13) $\frac{2}{3} - \frac{2}{5} =$

14) $\frac{3}{4} - \frac{1}{5} =$

15) $\frac{4}{5} - \frac{1}{5} =$

16) $\frac{2}{3} - \frac{1}{2} =$

17) $\frac{2}{3} - \frac{2}{3} =$

18) $\frac{3}{5} - \frac{1}{3} =$

19) $\frac{1}{2} - \frac{2}{5} =$

20) $\frac{4}{5} - \frac{3}{5} =$

21) $\frac{4}{5} - \frac{1}{2} =$

22) $\frac{2}{5} - \frac{1}{3} =$

23) $\frac{2}{3} - \frac{1}{2} =$

24) $\frac{2}{3} - \frac{2}{5} =$

25) $\frac{2}{3} - \frac{1}{2} =$

26) $\frac{3}{4} - \frac{1}{2} =$

27) $\frac{1}{2} - \frac{2}{5} =$

28) $\frac{1}{3} - \frac{1}{3} =$

29) $\frac{2}{3} - \frac{1}{2} =$

30) $\frac{4}{5} - \frac{2}{3} =$

1) $\frac{1}{2} - \frac{1}{3} =$

2) $\frac{2}{5} - \frac{1}{4} =$

3) $\frac{1}{2} - \frac{1}{2} =$

4) $\frac{3}{4} - \frac{1}{2} =$

5) $\frac{4}{5} - \frac{4}{5} =$

6) $\frac{4}{5} - \frac{1}{4} =$

7) $\frac{1}{3} - \frac{1}{3} =$

8) $\frac{4}{5} - \frac{1}{2} =$

9) $\frac{1}{2} - \frac{1}{2} =$

10) $\frac{3}{4} - \frac{1}{5} =$

11) $\frac{1}{2} - \frac{1}{5} =$

12) $\frac{3}{4} - \frac{2}{5} =$

13) $\frac{1}{3} - \frac{1}{3} =$

14) $\frac{3}{4} - \frac{3}{5} =$

15) $\frac{1}{2} - \frac{2}{5} =$

16) $\frac{1}{2} - \frac{1}{5} =$

17) $\frac{3}{4} - \frac{1}{2} =$

18) $\frac{2}{3} - \frac{1}{2} =$

19) $\frac{1}{2} - \frac{1}{5} =$

20) $\frac{2}{3} - \frac{1}{2} =$

21) $\frac{4}{5} - \frac{1}{2} =$

22) $\frac{2}{5} - \frac{1}{4} =$

23) $\frac{1}{2} - \frac{1}{5} =$

24) $\frac{3}{4} - \frac{1}{2} =$

25) $\frac{1}{2} - \frac{2}{5} =$

26) $\frac{4}{5} - \frac{1}{5} =$

27) $\frac{2}{5} - \frac{1}{3} =$

28) $\frac{3}{4} - \frac{1}{3} =$

29) $\frac{2}{3} - \frac{1}{2} =$

30) $\frac{1}{2} - \frac{1}{2} =$

25/42

⅓

1) $\frac{23}{6} - 2 =$

2) $\frac{10}{3} - \frac{6}{5} =$

3) $\frac{24}{5} - \frac{17}{6} =$

4) $2 - \frac{4}{3} =$

5) $\frac{9}{2} - \frac{25}{8} =$

6) $\frac{22}{7} - \frac{4}{3} =$

7) $\frac{7}{2} - \frac{27}{8} =$

8) $\frac{14}{3} - \frac{13}{5} =$

9) $\frac{23}{6} - \frac{1}{8} =$

10) $\frac{12}{5} - \frac{1}{3} =$

11) $\frac{17}{4} - \frac{5}{2} =$

12) $\frac{9}{2} - \frac{6}{5} =$

13) $\frac{14}{3} - \frac{1}{3} =$

14) $\frac{15}{8} - 1 =$

15) $5 - \frac{26}{7} =$

16) $\frac{13}{4} - 1 =$

17) $\frac{3}{2} - \frac{7}{6} =$

18) $3 - \frac{13}{6} =$

19) $\frac{34}{7} - 2 =$

20) $2 - \frac{1}{4} =$

21) $\frac{7}{2} - 1 =$

22) $\frac{39}{8} - \frac{1}{2} =$

23) $\frac{5}{3} - 1 =$

24) $\frac{15}{4} - \frac{11}{6} =$

25) $\frac{1}{4} - \frac{1}{7} =$

26) $\frac{25}{8} - \frac{11}{5} =$

27) $2 - \frac{2}{5} =$

28) $3 - \frac{7}{3} =$

29) $\frac{5}{3} - \frac{9}{7} =$

30) $3 - \frac{7}{3} =$

1) $\frac{11}{4} - \frac{17}{7} =$

2) $\frac{17}{4} - 4 =$

3) $\frac{23}{6} - \frac{7}{2} =$

4) $5 - \frac{5}{3} =$

5) $\frac{30}{7} - \frac{1}{2} =$

6) $3 - \frac{11}{4} =$

7) $\frac{13}{6} - \frac{1}{8} =$

8) $\frac{17}{5} - \frac{5}{2} =$

9) $5 - \frac{17}{5} =$

10) $\frac{14}{3} - \frac{5}{7} =$

11) $\frac{25}{6} - \frac{4}{3} =$

12) $5 - \frac{7}{5} =$

13) $\frac{15}{4} - \frac{26}{7} =$

14) $\frac{13}{3} - 3 =$

15) $\frac{7}{4} - \frac{4}{7} =$

16) $\frac{15}{4} - \frac{7}{3} =$

17) $\frac{11}{3} - 2 =$

18) $\frac{5}{2} - \frac{5}{3} =$

19) $\frac{7}{4} - 1 =$

20) $3 - \frac{5}{2} =$

21) $\frac{34}{7} - \frac{1}{8} =$

22) $\frac{26}{7} - \frac{19}{6} =$

23) $\frac{14}{3} - \frac{9}{2} =$

24) $2 - \frac{3}{2} =$

25) $4 - \frac{13}{6} =$

26) $\frac{31}{7} - \frac{11}{5} =$

27) $\frac{15}{4} - \frac{16}{7} =$

28) $\frac{11}{8} - \frac{3}{5} =$

29) $\frac{9}{2} - \frac{5}{3} =$

30) $\frac{13}{6} - \frac{6}{5} =$

27/42

$\frac{1}{3}$

1) $\frac{32}{7} - 1 =$

2) $\frac{3}{2} - \frac{5}{4} =$

3) $\frac{5}{2} - \frac{1}{2} =$

4) $4 - \frac{3}{2} =$

5) $\frac{14}{3} - \frac{11}{8} =$

6) $\frac{11}{7} - \frac{11}{8} =$

7) $\frac{29}{8} - \frac{1}{4} =$

8) $4 - \frac{14}{5} =$

9) $3 - \frac{7}{8} =$

10) $\frac{17}{4} - \frac{25}{6} =$

11) $\frac{13}{3} - \frac{5}{3} =$

12) $\frac{5}{2} - \frac{7}{8} =$

13) $\frac{5}{3} - \frac{1}{2} =$

14) $\frac{13}{4} - \frac{1}{2} =$

15) $\frac{13}{3} - \frac{1}{5} =$

16) $\frac{30}{7} - \frac{1}{2} =$

17) $\frac{7}{5} - \frac{1}{5} =$

18) $\frac{11}{5} - \frac{1}{6} =$

19) $\frac{10}{3} - \frac{1}{2} =$

20) $\frac{10}{3} - \frac{4}{3} =$

21) $3 - \frac{3}{4} =$

22) $\frac{11}{4} - 2 =$

23) $\frac{14}{3} - 2 =$

24) $\frac{26}{7} - \frac{11}{3} =$

25) $\frac{8}{3} - \frac{13}{8} =$

26) $5 - \frac{7}{5} =$

27) $\frac{7}{3} - 2 =$

28) $5 - \frac{23}{8} =$

29) $\frac{5}{2} - \frac{13}{7} =$

30) $3 - \frac{3}{4} =$

28/42

⅓

1) $\frac{29}{6} - 2 =$

2) $\frac{31}{8} - \frac{11}{6} =$

3) $\frac{21}{5} - \frac{17}{8} =$

4) $\frac{25}{7} - \frac{13}{5} =$

5) $\frac{19}{4} - \frac{11}{3} =$

6) $\frac{14}{3} - \frac{31}{8} =$

7) $\frac{21}{5} - \frac{9}{4} =$

8) $\frac{27}{8} - \frac{17}{8} =$

9) $\frac{5}{2} - \frac{9}{4} =$

10) $\frac{30}{7} - \frac{8}{3} =$

11) $\frac{31}{7} - \frac{19}{8} =$

12) $\frac{21}{5} - \frac{5}{2} =$

13) $3 - \frac{15}{7} =$

14) $\frac{21}{5} - 2 =$

15) $\frac{13}{6} - \frac{7}{4} =$

16) $4 - \frac{7}{2} =$

17) $\frac{5}{3} - \frac{1}{3} =$

18) $\frac{15}{4} - \frac{6}{7} =$

19) $\frac{13}{3} - \frac{3}{2} =$

20) $\frac{10}{3} - \frac{2}{3} =$

21) $\frac{35}{8} - \frac{18}{7} =$

22) $\frac{7}{4} - \frac{13}{8} =$

23) $3 - \frac{19}{7} =$

24) $2 - \frac{1}{2} =$

25) $\frac{23}{8} - \frac{2}{5} =$

26) $5 - \frac{16}{5} =$

27) $4 - \frac{18}{5} =$

28) $\frac{9}{2} - \frac{7}{2} =$

29) $\frac{2}{3} - \frac{5}{8} =$

30) $\frac{5}{3} - \frac{3}{2} =$

1) $\frac{26}{5} - \frac{31}{6} =$

2) $\frac{7}{2} - \frac{1}{3} =$

3) $\frac{9}{4} - \frac{1}{2} =$

4) $\frac{9}{2} - 4 =$

5) $5 - \frac{29}{7} =$

6) $\frac{11}{4} - \frac{5}{3} =$

7) $\frac{7}{2} - 3 =$

8) $\frac{19}{4} - \frac{5}{3} =$

9) $\frac{1}{2} - \frac{2}{5} =$

10) $\frac{11}{2} - \frac{9}{2} =$

11) $\frac{32}{7} - \frac{9}{5} =$

12) $\frac{9}{2} - 1 =$

13) $\frac{7}{2} - \frac{5}{4} =$

14) $\frac{8}{3} - \frac{3}{2} =$

15) $5 - \frac{21}{8} =$

16) $\frac{23}{5} - \frac{7}{3} =$

17) $\frac{11}{3} - \frac{1}{4} =$

18) $\frac{18}{7} - \frac{7}{3} =$

19) $\frac{14}{3} - \frac{9}{2} =$

20) $\frac{22}{5} - 3 =$

21) $3 - \frac{2}{5} =$

22) $\frac{17}{4} - \frac{10}{3} =$

23) $\frac{3}{2} - 1 =$

24) $\frac{9}{2} - \frac{12}{7} =$

25) $3 - \frac{1}{4} =$

26) $\frac{3}{2} - 1 =$

27) $\frac{29}{7} - \frac{7}{5} =$

28) $\frac{24}{7} - \frac{10}{3} =$

29) $2 - \frac{7}{4} =$

30) $\frac{5}{2} - \frac{3}{2} =$

Adding and Subtracting Fractions

1) $\frac{2}{3} + \frac{1}{2} =$

2) $\frac{3}{4} - \frac{1}{4} =$

3) $\frac{1}{2} - \frac{1}{3} =$

4) $\frac{1}{3} + \frac{1}{4} =$

5) $\frac{1}{2} + \frac{1}{2} =$

6) $\frac{2}{3} - \frac{3}{5} =$

7) $\frac{1}{2} + \frac{1}{2} =$

8) $1 - \frac{1}{5} =$

9) $\frac{2}{3} + \frac{2}{5} =$

10) $\frac{4}{5} + \frac{1}{2} =$

11) $\frac{2}{3} - \frac{1}{2} =$

12) $\frac{4}{5} - \frac{1}{3} =$

13) $\frac{4}{5} - \frac{2}{5} =$

14) $\frac{1}{5} + \frac{1}{3} =$

15) $\frac{1}{2} - \frac{2}{5} =$

16) $\frac{1}{3} + \frac{1}{2} =$

17) $\frac{1}{2} + \frac{1}{2} =$

18) $\frac{3}{4} + \frac{1}{3} =$

19) $\frac{1}{2} - \frac{1}{3} =$

20) $\frac{1}{4} - \frac{1}{4} =$

21) $\frac{3}{4} - \frac{3}{5} =$

22) $\frac{3}{5} + \frac{1}{2} =$

23) $\frac{3}{4} - \frac{1}{4} =$

24) $\frac{1}{2} + \frac{1}{2} =$

25) $\frac{2}{5} - \frac{1}{4} =$

26) $\frac{3}{4} + \frac{1}{2} =$

27) $\frac{2}{3} - \frac{2}{3} =$

28) $\frac{1}{3} + \frac{3}{5} =$

29) $\frac{3}{4} - \frac{1}{2} =$

30) $\frac{1}{2} - \frac{1}{2} =$

1) $\frac{1}{2} - \frac{2}{5} =$

2) $\frac{1}{2} - \frac{1}{5} =$

3) $\frac{2}{3} + \frac{1}{2} =$

4) $\frac{3}{4} + \frac{4}{5} =$

5) $\frac{3}{5} - \frac{1}{4} =$

6) $\frac{1}{2} + \frac{2}{3} =$

7) $\frac{2}{5} + \frac{1}{2} =$

8) $\frac{3}{4} - \frac{1}{2} =$

9) $\frac{3}{5} - \frac{1}{5} =$

10) $\frac{1}{2} + \frac{3}{5} =$

11) $\frac{3}{5} - \frac{1}{2} =$

12) $\frac{1}{4} + \frac{1}{2} =$

13) $\frac{2}{3} + \frac{1}{3} =$

14) $\frac{1}{2} - \frac{1}{2} =$

15) $\frac{3}{4} - \frac{1}{2} =$

16) $\frac{1}{3} + \frac{1}{2} =$

17) $\frac{1}{3} + \frac{2}{3} =$

18) $\frac{1}{2} - \frac{2}{5} =$

19) $\frac{1}{5} + \frac{2}{3} =$

20) $\frac{3}{5} - \frac{1}{4} =$

21) $\frac{2}{3} - \frac{2}{3} =$

22) $1 - \frac{3}{5} =$

23) $\frac{2}{5} + \frac{1}{2} =$

24) $\frac{4}{5} + \frac{1}{3} =$

25) $\frac{1}{2} + \frac{1}{2} =$

26) $\frac{2}{3} - \frac{2}{3} =$

27) $\frac{3}{4} - \frac{1}{2} =$

28) $\frac{4}{5} + \frac{1}{2} =$

29) $\frac{3}{4} - \frac{3}{5} =$

30) $\frac{2}{3} + \frac{1}{2} =$

32/42

$\frac{1}{3}$

1) $\frac{2}{3} - \frac{1}{2} =$

2) $\frac{2}{3} + \frac{2}{3} =$

3) $\frac{1}{3} + \frac{3}{5} =$

4) $\frac{2}{5} - \frac{2}{5} =$

5) $\frac{3}{4} + \frac{1}{5} =$

6) $\frac{1}{4} + \frac{2}{3} =$

7) $\frac{3}{4} - \frac{1}{4} =$

8) $\frac{1}{2} - \frac{1}{2} =$

9) $\frac{2}{5} - \frac{1}{4} =$

10) $\frac{2}{3} - \frac{1}{2} =$

11) $\frac{4}{5} + \frac{1}{2} =$

12) $\frac{1}{4} + \frac{1}{2} =$

13) $\frac{1}{3} + \frac{1}{3} =$

14) $\frac{1}{2} - \frac{1}{3} =$

15) $\frac{1}{2} + \frac{2}{3} =$

16) $\frac{2}{3} - \frac{1}{2} =$

17) $\frac{1}{4} + \frac{2}{3} =$

18) $\frac{1}{2} + \frac{1}{4} =$

19) $\frac{2}{3} - \frac{1}{4} =$

20) $\frac{1}{2} - \frac{1}{5} =$

21) $\frac{3}{5} - \frac{1}{3} =$

22) $\frac{2}{3} - \frac{2}{3} =$

23) $\frac{3}{4} + \frac{1}{2} =$

24) $\frac{1}{3} + \frac{2}{5} =$

25) $\frac{3}{5} + \frac{3}{4} =$

26) $\frac{1}{2} + \frac{1}{2} =$

27) $\frac{3}{4} - \frac{2}{3} =$

28) $\frac{1}{2} - \frac{1}{3} =$

29) $\frac{3}{4} + \frac{1}{2} =$

30) $\frac{2}{5} - \frac{1}{4} =$

1) $\frac{1}{3} - \frac{1}{4} =$

2) $\frac{1}{3} + \frac{2}{3} =$

3) $\frac{3}{4} - \frac{1}{2} =$

4) $\frac{1}{2} + \frac{1}{2} =$

5) $\frac{4}{5} - \frac{1}{3} =$

6) $\frac{3}{4} - \frac{2}{5} =$

7) $\frac{4}{5} + \frac{1}{2} =$

8) $\frac{1}{4} + \frac{1}{2} =$

9) $\frac{3}{4} + \frac{1}{2} =$

10) $\frac{2}{3} - \frac{1}{2} =$

11) $\frac{1}{2} - \frac{1}{2} =$

12) $\frac{1}{4} + \frac{1}{2} =$

13) $\frac{1}{2} + \frac{3}{5} =$

14) $\frac{1}{2} + \frac{1}{2} =$

15) $\frac{3}{5} - \frac{1}{2} =$

16) $\frac{1}{2} - \frac{1}{4} =$

17) $\frac{2}{3} - \frac{2}{3} =$

18) $\frac{1}{3} + \frac{1}{4} =$

19) $\frac{4}{5} - \frac{3}{4} =$

20) $\frac{1}{2} + \frac{1}{2} =$

21) $\frac{3}{5} + \frac{1}{2} =$

22) $\frac{1}{2} - \frac{1}{4} =$

23) $\frac{2}{3} + \frac{4}{5} =$

24) $\frac{4}{5} - \frac{1}{4} =$

25) $\frac{1}{2} + \frac{3}{5} =$

26) $\frac{2}{5} - \frac{1}{4} =$

27) $\frac{2}{3} + \frac{1}{3} =$

28) $\frac{3}{4} - \frac{1}{2} =$

29) $\frac{2}{3} - \frac{1}{2} =$

30) $\frac{4}{5} - \frac{1}{4} =$

1) $\frac{2}{5} + \frac{1}{2} =$

2) $\frac{2}{3} - \frac{1}{2} =$

3) $\frac{3}{4} - \frac{3}{5} =$

4) $\frac{4}{5} + \frac{2}{5} =$

5) $\frac{4}{5} - \frac{1}{2} =$

6) $\frac{3}{5} + \frac{1}{2} =$

7) $\frac{1}{2} + \frac{1}{4} =$

8) $\frac{3}{4} - \frac{1}{2} =$

9) $\frac{1}{2} - \frac{1}{5} =$

10) $\frac{2}{5} + \frac{1}{2} =$

11) $\frac{1}{5} + \frac{1}{2} =$

12) $\frac{1}{3} - \frac{1}{4} =$

13) $\frac{1}{2} + \frac{1}{2} =$

14) $\frac{3}{4} - \frac{3}{5} =$

15) $\frac{4}{5} + \frac{1}{4} =$

16) $1 - \frac{2}{3} =$

17) $\frac{1}{2} + \frac{1}{4} =$

18) $\frac{4}{5} - \frac{3}{4} =$

19) $\frac{1}{2} + \frac{1}{3} =$

20) $\frac{3}{4} - \frac{1}{3} =$

21) $\frac{3}{5} - \frac{1}{2} =$

22) $\frac{1}{3} + \frac{1}{2} =$

23) $\frac{4}{5} - \frac{2}{5} =$

24) $\frac{1}{5} + \frac{1}{2} =$

25) $\frac{1}{2} + \frac{2}{3} =$

26) $\frac{2}{3} - \frac{1}{4} =$

27) $\frac{4}{5} + \frac{1}{2} =$

28) $\frac{2}{3} - \frac{1}{2} =$

29) $\frac{1}{4} + \frac{1}{2} =$

30) $\frac{1}{2} - \frac{1}{2} =$

1) $\frac{16}{3} - \frac{9}{4} =$

2) $\frac{5}{4} + \frac{23}{7} =$

3) $\frac{11}{4} + \frac{1}{4} =$

4) $2 - \frac{8}{7} =$

5) $4 + \frac{9}{2} =$

6) $\frac{7}{2} - \frac{4}{3} =$

7) $3 - \frac{3}{2} =$

8) $\frac{9}{2} + \frac{34}{7} =$

9) $\frac{3}{2} - 1 =$

10) $\frac{7}{6} + \frac{39}{8} =$

11) $2 - \frac{1}{4} =$

12) $\frac{4}{3} + \frac{11}{3} =$

13) $\frac{10}{3} - \frac{7}{3} =$

14) $\frac{29}{6} - 1 =$

15) $4 + \frac{3}{2} =$

16) $\frac{1}{2} + \frac{25}{6} =$

17) $5 - \frac{29}{8} =$

18) $\frac{7}{3} + 2 =$

19) $\frac{3}{2} + 1 =$

20) $\frac{7}{2} - \frac{7}{3} =$

21) $\frac{19}{4} - 4 =$

22) $\frac{31}{8} + \frac{25}{8} =$

23) $\frac{5}{2} + 3 =$

24) $4 - \frac{2}{3} =$

25) $\frac{16}{5} + 1 =$

26) $\frac{19}{4} - 4 =$

27) $\frac{5}{2} - \frac{13}{7} =$

28) $\frac{7}{2} + \frac{7}{2} =$

29) $\frac{13}{3} - \frac{9}{8} =$

30) $\frac{17}{6} + \frac{25}{6} =$

36/42

1) $\frac{13}{8} + \frac{9}{2} =$

2) $\frac{10}{3} + \frac{21}{5} =$

3) $\frac{5}{2} - 2 =$

4) $\frac{31}{7} - \frac{2}{7} =$

5) $\frac{29}{6} - 3 =$

6) $\frac{27}{7} - \frac{5}{2} =$

7) $\frac{7}{6} + \frac{24}{5} =$

8) $\frac{15}{4} + \frac{10}{3} =$

9) $\frac{13}{5} - \frac{5}{3} =$

10) $\frac{9}{7} + \frac{15}{8} =$

11) $\frac{22}{5} - 2 =$

12) $\frac{16}{7} + 1 =$

13) $\frac{4}{5} + 3 =$

14) $1 + \frac{17}{4} =$

15) $\frac{7}{2} - \frac{1}{7} =$

16) $5 - \frac{1}{3} =$

17) $\frac{2}{3} + \frac{13}{3} =$

18) $\frac{8}{7} - 1 =$

19) $4 + \frac{31}{6} =$

20) $\frac{29}{8} - \frac{11}{4} =$

21) $4 - \frac{5}{7} =$

22) $2 + \frac{18}{7} =$

23) $\frac{7}{2} - \frac{3}{4} =$

24) $\frac{4}{3} + \frac{7}{4} =$

25) $\frac{21}{4} - \frac{7}{6} =$

26) $\frac{14}{3} - \frac{11}{8} =$

27) $\frac{9}{4} + \frac{3}{2} =$

28) $\frac{26}{7} + \frac{13}{3} =$

29) $\frac{11}{5} + 2 =$

30) $\frac{13}{4} - \frac{3}{2} =$

37/42

⅓

1) $\frac{8}{3} - \frac{2}{5} =$

2) $\frac{8}{7} + 5 =$

3) $\frac{11}{2} - 3 =$

4) $\frac{11}{7} + \frac{13}{5} =$

5) $5 - \frac{11}{8} =$

6) $\frac{24}{5} - \frac{2}{7} =$

7) $\frac{7}{2} + 3 =$

8) $\frac{13}{3} + 5 =$

9) $\frac{2}{7} + 4 =$

10) $\frac{5}{8} - \frac{2}{5} =$

11) $\frac{3}{4} - \frac{2}{3} =$

12) $\frac{5}{2} + \frac{4}{3} =$

13) $\frac{29}{8} - \frac{11}{7} =$

14) $\frac{4}{3} + \frac{5}{2} =$

15) $\frac{6}{7} + \frac{14}{3} =$

16) $\frac{7}{2} - \frac{8}{3} =$

17) $\frac{9}{2} - \frac{4}{7} =$

18) $\frac{3}{2} + \frac{1}{2} =$

19) $\frac{5}{2} + \frac{2}{3} =$

20) $4 - \frac{18}{5} =$

21) $\frac{3}{2} - \frac{2}{3} =$

22) $\frac{25}{8} + \frac{5}{4} =$

23) $\frac{7}{3} - \frac{5}{6} =$

24) $1 + \frac{9}{2} =$

25) $\frac{33}{8} + \frac{8}{7} =$

26) $\frac{19}{6} - \frac{3}{8} =$

27) $\frac{25}{8} - \frac{5}{3} =$

28) $\frac{25}{7} + \frac{11}{3} =$

29) $\frac{26}{7} + \frac{9}{2} =$

30) $\frac{13}{3} - 2 =$

1) $\frac{1}{3} + \frac{11}{4} =$

2) $\frac{1}{2} + \frac{4}{3} =$

3) $\frac{14}{3} - 4 =$

4) $\frac{19}{5} - \frac{5}{2} =$

5) $\frac{5}{8} + \frac{3}{4} =$

6) $5 + \frac{1}{4} =$

7) $\frac{23}{6} - 1 =$

8) $\frac{29}{6} - \frac{9}{2} =$

9) $\frac{9}{2} - \frac{12}{5} =$

10) $3 - \frac{11}{6} =$

11) $\frac{13}{4} + \frac{5}{4} =$

12) $\frac{2}{7} + 4 =$

13) $\frac{23}{6} - \frac{25}{7} =$

14) $\frac{7}{2} - \frac{1}{6} =$

15) $\frac{10}{3} + 1 =$

16) $\frac{8}{3} + \frac{31}{8} =$

17) $\frac{22}{5} + \frac{17}{4} =$

39/42

18) $\frac{2}{3} + \frac{3}{2} =$

19) $\frac{17}{5} - \frac{1}{2} =$

20) $\frac{33}{7} - \frac{14}{3} =$

21) $4 + \frac{31}{7} =$

22) $\frac{5}{2} - \frac{2}{5} =$

23) $\frac{5}{2} + \frac{9}{2} =$

24) $\frac{19}{4} - \frac{19}{6} =$

25) $\frac{25}{8} - 3 =$

26) $4 + \frac{5}{6} =$

27) $3 + \frac{13}{5} =$

28) $\frac{9}{2} - \frac{8}{5} =$

29) $1 + \frac{13}{4} =$

30) $3 - \frac{3}{2} =$

1) $\frac{11}{5} + \frac{7}{4} =$

2) $\frac{10}{7} + \frac{22}{7} =$

3) $\frac{14}{3} - 2 =$

4) $4 - \frac{3}{2} =$

5) $\frac{13}{3} - \frac{8}{3} =$

6) $2 + \frac{7}{2} =$

7) $\frac{5}{2} - \frac{11}{5} =$

8) $\frac{9}{5} + \frac{9}{2} =$

9) $\frac{1}{2} + \frac{5}{4} =$

10) $1 + \frac{13}{4} =$

11) $5 - \frac{20}{7} =$

12) $\frac{15}{4} - \frac{1}{4} =$

13) $\frac{7}{2} - \frac{8}{5} =$

14) $\frac{9}{2} - \frac{31}{8} =$

15) $\frac{16}{5} + \frac{22}{7} =$

16) $\frac{14}{3} + \frac{5}{2} =$

17) $\frac{2}{5} + \frac{29}{6} =$

18) $3 - \frac{13}{5} =$

19) $\frac{21}{5} + \frac{19}{6} =$

20) $\frac{7}{3} - \frac{2}{3} =$

21) $\frac{3}{2} + \frac{15}{4} =$

22) $\frac{3}{2} - \frac{1}{7} =$

23) $1 + \frac{3}{5} =$

24) $\frac{9}{2} - 4 =$

25) $3 + \frac{1}{4} =$

26) $\frac{5}{3} + \frac{13}{4} =$

27) $\frac{1}{3} - \frac{1}{3} =$

28) $\frac{16}{3} - \frac{9}{2} =$

29) $\frac{23}{5} + \frac{14}{3} =$

30) $\frac{18}{7} - 1 =$

Answers

1) $\frac{1}{3}$ of 12 = **4**   2) $\frac{1}{2}$ of 10 = **5**   3) $\frac{1}{3}$ of 15 = **5**

4) $\frac{1}{3}$ of 0 = **0**   5) $\frac{1}{2}$ of 8 = **4**   6) $\frac{1}{4}$ of 12 = **3**

7) $\frac{1}{3}$ of 6 = **2**   8) $\frac{1}{4}$ of 20 = **5**   9) $\frac{1}{3}$ of 12 = **4**

10) $\frac{1}{3}$ of 9 = **3**   11) $\frac{1}{3}$ of 6 = **2**   12) $\frac{1}{4}$ of 16 = **4**

13) $\frac{1}{2}$ of 4 = **2**   14) $\frac{1}{3}$ of 12 = **4**   15) $\frac{1}{2}$ of 8 = **4**

16) $\frac{1}{2}$ of 10 = **5**   17) $\frac{1}{2}$ of 8 = **4**   18) $\frac{1}{3}$ of 12 = **4**

19) $\frac{1}{2}$ of 6 = **3**   20) $\frac{1}{3}$ of 12 = **4**   21) $\frac{1}{3}$ of 12 = **4**

22) $\frac{1}{4}$ of 12 = **3**   23) $\frac{1}{3}$ of 15 = **5**   24) $\frac{1}{3}$ of 15 = **5**

25) $\frac{1}{3}$ of 6 = **2**   26) $\frac{1}{4}$ of 16 = **4**   27) $\frac{1}{2}$ of 4 = **2**

28) $\frac{1}{2}$ of 0 = **0**   29) $\frac{1}{3}$ of 3 = **1**   30) $\frac{1}{2}$ of 2 = **1**

1) $\frac{1}{3}$ of 12 = **4**

2) $\frac{1}{4}$ of 4 = **1**

3) $\frac{1}{3}$ of 3 = **1**

4) $\frac{1}{2}$ of 8 = **4**

5) $\frac{1}{3}$ of 9 = **3**

6) $\frac{1}{4}$ of 8 = **2**

7) $\frac{1}{4}$ of 8 = **2**

8) $\frac{1}{3}$ of 9 = **3**

9) $\frac{1}{2}$ of 8 = **4**

10) $\frac{1}{3}$ of 3 = **1**

11) $\frac{1}{3}$ of 6 = **2**

12) $\frac{1}{3}$ of 9 = **3**

13) $\frac{1}{2}$ of 4 = **2**

14) $\frac{1}{3}$ of 6 = **2**

15) $\frac{1}{3}$ of 6 = **2**

16) $\frac{1}{4}$ of 16 = **4**

17) $\frac{1}{2}$ of 2 = **1**

18) $\frac{1}{2}$ of 6 = **3**

19) $\frac{1}{2}$ of 8 = **4**

20) $\frac{1}{4}$ of 8 = **2**

21) $\frac{1}{3}$ of 15 = **5**

22) $\frac{1}{4}$ of 12 = **3**

23) $\frac{1}{3}$ of 12 = **4**

24) $\frac{1}{3}$ of 6 = **2**

25) $\frac{1}{3}$ of 15 = **5**

26) $\frac{1}{4}$ of 12 = **3**

27) $\frac{1}{4}$ of 20 = **5**

28) $\frac{1}{3}$ of 9 = **3**

29) $\frac{1}{3}$ of 3 = **1**

30) $\frac{1}{4}$ of 12 = **3**

1) $\frac{1}{3}$ of 12 = **4**

2) $\frac{1}{3}$ of 3 = **1**

3) $\frac{1}{4}$ of 4 = **1**

4) $\frac{1}{3}$ of 9 = **3**

5) $\frac{1}{4}$ of 12 = **3**

6) $\frac{1}{2}$ of 10 = **5**

7) $\frac{1}{3}$ of 15 = **5**

8) $\frac{1}{2}$ of 6 = **3**

9) $\frac{1}{2}$ of 10 = **5**

10) $\frac{1}{4}$ of 12 = **3**

11) $\frac{1}{2}$ of 2 = **1**

12) $\frac{1}{4}$ of 0 = **0**

13) $\frac{1}{3}$ of 12 = **4**

14) $\frac{1}{2}$ of 2 = **1**

15) $\frac{1}{4}$ of 4 = **1**

16) $\frac{1}{2}$ of 8 = **4**

17) $\frac{1}{2}$ of 8 = **4**

18) $\frac{1}{3}$ of 3 = **1**

19) $\frac{1}{2}$ of 8 = **4**

20) $\frac{1}{4}$ of 16 = **4**

21) $\frac{1}{4}$ of 16 = **4**

22) $\frac{1}{4}$ of 8 = **2**

23) $\frac{1}{4}$ of 12 = **3**

24) $\frac{1}{2}$ of 8 = **4**

25) $\frac{1}{4}$ of 20 = **5**

26) $\frac{1}{3}$ of 12 = **4**

27) $\frac{1}{3}$ of 12 = **4**

28) $\frac{1}{3}$ of 6 = **2**

29) $\frac{1}{4}$ of 12 = **3**

30) $\frac{1}{4}$ of 20 = **5**

1) $\frac{1}{4}$ of 12 = **3**

2) $\frac{1}{4}$ of 20 = **5**

3) $\frac{1}{2}$ of 8 = **4**

4) $\frac{1}{2}$ of 10 = **5**

5) $\frac{1}{2}$ of 10 = **5**

6) $\frac{1}{2}$ of 2 = **1**

7) $\frac{1}{3}$ of 3 = **1**

8) $\frac{1}{2}$ of 10 = **5**

9) $\frac{1}{2}$ of 8 = **4**

10) $\frac{1}{4}$ of 12 = **3**

11) $\frac{1}{3}$ of 6 = **2**

12) $\frac{1}{4}$ of 12 = **3**

13) $\frac{1}{4}$ of 12 = **3**

14) $\frac{1}{2}$ of 10 = **5**

15) $\frac{1}{2}$ of 4 = **2**

16) $\frac{1}{2}$ of 4 = **2**

17) $\frac{1}{2}$ of 10 = **5**

18) $\frac{1}{3}$ of 15 = **5**

19) $\frac{1}{2}$ of 10 = **5**

20) $\frac{1}{3}$ of 15 = **5**

21) $\frac{1}{4}$ of 4 = **1**

22) $\frac{1}{3}$ of 6 = **2**

23) $\frac{1}{4}$ of 20 = **5**

24) $\frac{1}{2}$ of 10 = **5**

25) $\frac{1}{2}$ of 6 = **3**

26) $\frac{1}{4}$ of 4 = **1**

27) $\frac{1}{3}$ of 3 = **1**

28) $\frac{1}{2}$ of 10 = **5**

29) $\frac{1}{3}$ of 0 = **0**

30) $\frac{1}{4}$ of 4 = **1**

1) $\frac{1}{2}$ of 10 = **5**

2) $\frac{1}{2}$ of 2 = **1**

3) $\frac{1}{4}$ of 16 = **4**

4) $\frac{1}{4}$ of 4 = **1**

5) $\frac{1}{2}$ of 4 = **2**

6) $\frac{1}{2}$ of 4 = **2**

7) $\frac{1}{4}$ of 20 = **5**

8) $\frac{1}{2}$ of 6 = **3**

9) $\frac{1}{4}$ of 16 = **4**

10) $\frac{1}{4}$ of 4 = **1**

11) $\frac{1}{2}$ of 4 = **2**

12) $\frac{1}{2}$ of 4 = **2**

13) $\frac{1}{3}$ of 6 = **2**

14) $\frac{1}{2}$ of 4 = **2**

15) $\frac{1}{3}$ of 9 = **3**

16) $\frac{1}{2}$ of 4 = **2**

17) $\frac{1}{3}$ of 9 = **3**

18) $\frac{1}{2}$ of 6 = **3**

19) $\frac{1}{3}$ of 3 = **1**

20) $\frac{1}{4}$ of 4 = **1**

21) $\frac{1}{2}$ of 8 = **4**

22) $\frac{1}{4}$ of 20 = **5**

23) $\frac{1}{2}$ of 2 = **1**

24) $\frac{1}{4}$ of 20 = **5**

25) $\frac{1}{4}$ of 8 = **2**

26) $\frac{1}{4}$ of 12 = **3**

27) $\frac{1}{3}$ of 12 = **4**

28) $\frac{1}{3}$ of 9 = **3**

29) $\frac{1}{4}$ of 12 = **3**

30) $\frac{1}{3}$ of 15 = **5**

1) $\frac{1}{3}$ of 3 = **1**

2) $\frac{1}{2}$ of 8 = **4**

3) $\frac{1}{3}$ of 15 = **5**

4) $\frac{1}{3}$ of 6 = **2**

5) $\frac{1}{2}$ of 8 = **4**

6) $\frac{1}{4}$ of 16 = **4**

7) $\frac{1}{4}$ of 12 = **3**

8) $\frac{1}{3}$ of 15 = **5**

9) $\frac{1}{3}$ of 15 = **5**

10) $\frac{1}{2}$ of 8 = **4**

11) $\frac{1}{4}$ of 4 = **1**

12) $\frac{1}{4}$ of 20 = **5**

13) $\frac{1}{3}$ of 9 = **3**

14) $\frac{1}{4}$ of 4 = **1**

15) $\frac{1}{4}$ of 4 = **1**

16) $\frac{1}{3}$ of 9 = **3**

17) $\frac{1}{3}$ of 9 = **3**

18) $\frac{1}{3}$ of 12 = **4**

19) $\frac{1}{4}$ of 4 = **1**

20) $\frac{1}{3}$ of 15 = **5**

21) $\frac{1}{2}$ of 4 = **2**

22) $\frac{1}{2}$ of 8 = **4**

23) $\frac{1}{4}$ of 8 = **2**

24) $\frac{1}{4}$ of 8 = **2**

25) $\frac{1}{2}$ of 6 = **3**

26) $\frac{1}{3}$ of 12 = **4**

27) $\frac{1}{3}$ of 9 = **3**

28) $\frac{1}{3}$ of 9 = **3**

29) $\frac{1}{3}$ of 0 = **0**

30) $\frac{1}{4}$ of 4 = **1**

1) $\frac{1}{3}$ of 9 = **3**

2) $\frac{1}{4}$ of 4 = **1**

3) $\frac{1}{3}$ of 15 = **5**

4) $\frac{1}{3}$ of 3 = **1**

5) $\frac{1}{3}$ of 3 = **1**

6) $\frac{1}{2}$ of 10 = **5**

7) $\frac{1}{4}$ of 16 = **4**

8) $\frac{1}{4}$ of 8 = **2**

9) $\frac{1}{4}$ of 16 = **4**

10) $\frac{1}{3}$ of 6 = **2**

11) $\frac{1}{4}$ of 4 = **1**

12) $\frac{1}{2}$ of 10 = **5**

13) $\frac{1}{3}$ of 3 = **1**

14) $\frac{1}{4}$ of 8 = **2**

15) $\frac{1}{4}$ of 20 = **5**

16) $\frac{1}{3}$ of 12 = **4**

17) $\frac{1}{3}$ of 12 = **4**

18) $\frac{1}{4}$ of 20 = **5**

19) $\frac{1}{2}$ of 4 = **2**

20) $\frac{1}{2}$ of 6 = **3**

21) $\frac{1}{2}$ of 2 = **1**

22) $\frac{1}{2}$ of 8 = **4**

23) $\frac{1}{2}$ of 4 = **2**

24) $\frac{1}{4}$ of 16 = **4**

25) $\frac{1}{3}$ of 12 = **4**

26) $\frac{1}{3}$ of 12 = **4**

27) $\frac{1}{2}$ of 6 = **3**

28) $\frac{1}{2}$ of 8 = **4**

29) $\frac{1}{2}$ of 10 = **5**

30) $\frac{1}{2}$ of 8 = **4**

1) $\frac{1}{2}$ of 6 = **3**

2) $\frac{1}{3}$ of 9 = **3**

3) $\frac{1}{2}$ of 2 = **1**

4) $\frac{1}{4}$ of 4 = **1**

5) $\frac{1}{4}$ of 16 = **4**

6) $\frac{1}{4}$ of 12 = **3**

7) $\frac{1}{4}$ of 8 = **2**

8) $\frac{1}{4}$ of 12 = **3**

9) $\frac{1}{4}$ of 16 = **4**

10) $\frac{1}{4}$ of 8 = **2**

11) $\frac{1}{2}$ of 4 = **2**

12) $\frac{1}{2}$ of 10 = **5**

13) $\frac{1}{4}$ of 4 = **1**

14) $\frac{1}{3}$ of 6 = **2**

15) $\frac{1}{3}$ of 3 = **1**

16) $\frac{1}{2}$ of 8 = **4**

17) $\frac{1}{3}$ of 15 = **5**

18) $\frac{1}{2}$ of 4 = **2**

19) $\frac{1}{3}$ of 9 = **3**

20) $\frac{1}{3}$ of 9 = **3**

21) $\frac{1}{3}$ of 3 = **1**

22) $\frac{1}{3}$ of 12 = **4**

23) $\frac{1}{4}$ of 4 = **1**

24) $\frac{1}{2}$ of 4 = **2**

25) $\frac{1}{3}$ of 15 = **5**

26) $\frac{1}{3}$ of 3 = **1**

27) $\frac{1}{4}$ of 8 = **2**

28) $\frac{1}{3}$ of 9 = **3**

29) $\frac{1}{2}$ of 4 = **2**

30) $\frac{1}{3}$ of 6 = **2**

1) $\frac{1}{3}$ of 15 = **5**

2) $\frac{1}{4}$ of 8 = **2**

3) $\frac{1}{4}$ of 16 = **4**

4) $\frac{1}{4}$ of 12 = **3**

5) $\frac{1}{3}$ of 12 = **4**

6) $\frac{1}{4}$ of 4 = **1**

7) $\frac{1}{2}$ of 8 = **4**

8) $\frac{1}{2}$ of 2 = **1**

9) $\frac{1}{3}$ of 12 = **4**

10) $\frac{1}{4}$ of 16 = **4**

11) $\frac{1}{2}$ of 8 = **4**

12) $\frac{1}{2}$ of 6 = **3**

13) $\frac{1}{2}$ of 10 = **5**

14) $\frac{1}{3}$ of 9 = **3**

15) $\frac{1}{2}$ of 10 = **5**

16) $\frac{1}{4}$ of 16 = **4**

17) $\frac{1}{2}$ of 2 = **1**

18) $\frac{1}{4}$ of 0 = **0**

19) $\frac{1}{2}$ of 2 = **1**

20) $\frac{1}{3}$ of 12 = **4**

21) $\frac{1}{2}$ of 10 = **5**

22) $\frac{1}{2}$ of 4 = **2**

23) $\frac{1}{2}$ of 4 = **2**

24) $\frac{1}{4}$ of 4 = **1**

25) $\frac{1}{3}$ of 12 = **4**

26) $\frac{1}{4}$ of 16 = **4**

27) $\frac{1}{4}$ of 12 = **3**

28) $\frac{1}{3}$ of 6 = **2**

29) $\frac{1}{3}$ of 6 = **2**

30) $\frac{1}{3}$ of 9 = **3**

1) $\frac{1}{3}$ of 6 = **2**

2) $\frac{1}{2}$ of 4 = **2**

3) $\frac{1}{4}$ of 4 = **1**

4) $\frac{1}{3}$ of 15 = **5**

5) $\frac{1}{3}$ of 3 = **1**

6) $\frac{1}{2}$ of 8 = **4**

7) $\frac{1}{4}$ of 12 = **3**

8) $\frac{1}{4}$ of 16 = **4**

9) $\frac{1}{2}$ of 8 = **4**

10) $\frac{1}{4}$ of 8 = **2**

11) $\frac{1}{2}$ of 10 = **5**

12) $\frac{1}{3}$ of 12 = **4**

13) $\frac{1}{3}$ of 6 = **2**

14) $\frac{1}{3}$ of 12 = **4**

15) $\frac{1}{3}$ of 12 = **4**

16) $\frac{1}{2}$ of 4 = **2**

17) $\frac{1}{2}$ of 10 = **5**

18) $\frac{1}{3}$ of 3 = **1**

19) $\frac{1}{4}$ of 16 = **4**

20) $\frac{1}{4}$ of 20 = **5**

21) $\frac{1}{3}$ of 9 = **3**

22) $\frac{1}{4}$ of 20 = **5**

23) $\frac{1}{3}$ of 0 = **0**

24) $\frac{1}{2}$ of 8 = **4**

25) $\frac{1}{4}$ of 16 = **4**

26) $\frac{1}{2}$ of 6 = **3**

27) $\frac{1}{3}$ of 3 = **1**

28) $\frac{1}{2}$ of 8 = **4**

29) $\frac{1}{4}$ of 16 = **4**

30) $\frac{1}{2}$ of 4 = **2**

1) $\frac{1}{2} + \frac{1}{2} =$ **1**

2) $\frac{1}{3} + \frac{3}{4} = \frac{13}{12}$ **or** $1\frac{1}{12}$

3) $\frac{4}{5} + \frac{1}{2} = \frac{13}{10}$ **or** $1\frac{3}{10}$

4) $\frac{1}{4} + \frac{1}{2} = \frac{3}{4}$

5) $\frac{1}{4} + \frac{2}{3} = \frac{11}{12}$

6) $\frac{1}{2} + \frac{2}{5} = \frac{9}{10}$

7) $\frac{2}{3} + \frac{1}{3} =$ **1**

8) $\frac{1}{2} + \frac{1}{3} = \frac{5}{6}$

9) $\frac{2}{3} + \frac{3}{5} = \frac{19}{15}$ **or** $1\frac{4}{15}$

10) $\frac{3}{4} + \frac{1}{5} = \frac{19}{20}$

11) $\frac{2}{3} + \frac{1}{5} = \frac{13}{15}$

12) $\frac{1}{3} + \frac{1}{2} = \frac{5}{6}$

13) $\frac{4}{5} + \frac{1}{5} =$ **1**

14) $\frac{1}{5} + \frac{2}{3} = \frac{13}{15}$

15) $\frac{1}{2} + \frac{4}{5} = \frac{13}{10}$ **or** $1\frac{3}{10}$

16) $\frac{3}{4} + \frac{1}{3} = \frac{13}{12}$ **or** $1\frac{1}{12}$

17) $\frac{2}{5} + \frac{2}{3} = \frac{16}{15}$ **or** $1\frac{1}{15}$

11/42

18) $\frac{1}{2} + \frac{1}{2} =$ **1**

19) $\frac{1}{2} + \frac{2}{3} = \frac{7}{6}$ **or** $1\frac{1}{6}$

20) $\frac{1}{3} + \frac{1}{2} = \frac{5}{6}$

21) $\frac{1}{2} + \frac{2}{3} = \frac{7}{6}$ **or** $1\frac{1}{6}$

22) $\frac{1}{3} + \frac{1}{2} = \frac{5}{6}$

23) $\frac{1}{2} + \frac{1}{2} =$ **1**

24) $\frac{1}{5} + 1 = \frac{6}{5}$ **or** $1\frac{1}{5}$

25) $\frac{2}{3} + \frac{3}{4} = \frac{17}{12}$ **or** $1\frac{5}{12}$

26) $\frac{1}{2} + \frac{1}{4} = \frac{3}{4}$

27) $\frac{2}{3} + \frac{3}{5} = \frac{19}{15}$ **or** $1\frac{4}{15}$

28) $\frac{1}{3} + \frac{1}{2} = \frac{5}{6}$

29) $\frac{1}{5} + 1 = \frac{6}{5}$ **or** $1\frac{1}{5}$

30) $\frac{1}{3} + \frac{1}{2} = \frac{5}{6}$

1) $\frac{3}{5} + \frac{1}{2} = \frac{11}{10}$ **or** $1\frac{1}{10}$

2) $\frac{1}{2} + \frac{2}{5} = \frac{9}{10}$

3) $\frac{3}{5} + \frac{4}{5} = \frac{7}{5}$ **or** $1\frac{2}{5}$

4) $\frac{1}{4} + \frac{3}{5} = \frac{17}{20}$

5) $\frac{1}{3} + \frac{1}{2} = \frac{5}{6}$

6) $\frac{4}{5} + \frac{2}{3} = \frac{22}{15}$ **or** $1\frac{7}{15}$

7) $\frac{1}{4} + \frac{2}{3} = \frac{11}{12}$

8) $\frac{3}{5} + \frac{1}{2} = \frac{11}{10}$ **or** $1\frac{1}{10}$

9) $\frac{1}{3} + \frac{1}{4} = \frac{7}{12}$

10) $\frac{3}{4} + \frac{1}{5} = \frac{19}{20}$

11) $\frac{3}{4} + \frac{2}{5} = \frac{23}{20}$ **or** $1\frac{3}{20}$

12) $\frac{1}{4} + \frac{3}{5} = \frac{17}{20}$

13) $\frac{1}{3} + \frac{2}{5} = \frac{11}{15}$

14) $\frac{1}{4} + \frac{2}{3} = \frac{11}{12}$

15) $\frac{2}{3} + \frac{1}{2} = \frac{7}{6}$ **or** $1\frac{1}{6}$

16) $\frac{1}{2} + \frac{1}{2} = \mathbf{1}$

17) $\frac{2}{3} + \frac{1}{2} = \frac{7}{6}$ **or** $1\frac{1}{6}$

18) $\frac{1}{2} + \frac{1}{4} = \frac{3}{4}$

19) $\frac{1}{3} + \frac{4}{5} = \frac{17}{15}$ **or** $1\frac{2}{15}$

12/42

20) $\frac{2}{3} + \frac{1}{2} = \frac{7}{6}$ **or** $1\frac{1}{6}$

21) $\frac{1}{2} + \frac{1}{3} = \frac{5}{6}$

22) $\frac{1}{3} + \frac{1}{3} = \frac{2}{3}$

23) $\frac{3}{4} + \frac{1}{2} = \frac{5}{4}$ **or** $1\frac{1}{4}$

24) $\frac{2}{3} + \frac{1}{3} = \mathbf{1}$

25) $\frac{1}{2} + \frac{2}{3} = \frac{7}{6}$ **or** $1\frac{1}{6}$

26) $\frac{3}{4} + \frac{3}{4} = \frac{3}{2}$ **or** $1\frac{1}{2}$

27) $\frac{1}{2} + \frac{1}{2} = \mathbf{1}$

28) $\frac{2}{3} + \frac{1}{3} = \mathbf{1}$

29) $\frac{1}{3} + \frac{2}{5} = \frac{11}{15}$

30) $\frac{1}{2} + \frac{3}{4} = \frac{5}{4}$ **or** $1\frac{1}{4}$

1) $\frac{3}{5} + \frac{1}{3} = \frac{14}{15}$

2) $\frac{3}{4} + \frac{2}{5} = \frac{23}{20}$ **or** $1\frac{3}{20}$

3) $\frac{3}{5} + \frac{1}{3} = \frac{14}{15}$

4) $\frac{1}{2} + \frac{1}{5} = \frac{7}{10}$

5) $\frac{1}{3} + \frac{1}{2} = \frac{5}{6}$

6) $\frac{1}{2} + \frac{1}{4} = \frac{3}{4}$

7) $\frac{2}{3} + \frac{4}{5} = \frac{22}{15}$ **or** $1\frac{7}{15}$

8) $\frac{3}{4} + \frac{1}{2} = \frac{5}{4}$ **or** $1\frac{1}{4}$

9) $\frac{3}{4} + \frac{3}{4} = \frac{3}{2}$ **or** $1\frac{1}{2}$

10) $\frac{1}{2} + \frac{1}{2} = \mathbf{1}$

11) $\frac{1}{4} + \frac{1}{2} = \frac{3}{4}$

12) $\frac{2}{5} + \frac{1}{2} = \frac{9}{10}$

13) $\frac{1}{4} + \frac{2}{5} = \frac{13}{20}$

14) $\frac{1}{2} + \frac{3}{4} = \frac{5}{4}$ **or** $1\frac{1}{4}$

15) $\frac{3}{4} + \frac{1}{5} = \frac{19}{20}$

16) $\frac{1}{3} + \frac{3}{4} = \frac{13}{12}$ **or** $1\frac{1}{12}$

17) $\frac{1}{4} + \frac{1}{2} = \frac{3}{4}$

18) $\frac{2}{3} + \frac{2}{3} = \frac{4}{3}$ **or** $1\frac{1}{3}$

19) $\frac{1}{3} + \frac{4}{5} = \frac{17}{15}$ **or** $1\frac{2}{15}$

13/42

20) $\frac{1}{2} + \frac{1}{2} = \mathbf{1}$

21) $\frac{3}{4} + \frac{1}{2} = \frac{5}{4}$ **or** $1\frac{1}{4}$

22) $\frac{4}{5} + \frac{1}{2} = \frac{13}{10}$ **or** $1\frac{3}{10}$

23) $\frac{2}{3} + \frac{2}{3} = \frac{4}{3}$ **or** $1\frac{1}{3}$

24) $\frac{1}{2} + \frac{3}{4} = \frac{5}{4}$ **or** $1\frac{1}{4}$

25) $\frac{1}{4} + \frac{1}{3} = \frac{7}{12}$

26) $\frac{1}{2} + \frac{2}{5} = \frac{9}{10}$

27) $\frac{2}{3} + \frac{1}{2} = \frac{7}{6}$ **or** $1\frac{1}{6}$

28) $\frac{3}{5} + \frac{1}{2} = \frac{11}{10}$ **or** $1\frac{1}{10}$

29) $\frac{2}{3} + \frac{1}{2} = \frac{7}{6}$ **or** $1\frac{1}{6}$

30) $\frac{3}{5} + \frac{2}{3} = \frac{19}{15}$ **or** $1\frac{4}{15}$

1) $\frac{3}{4} + \frac{2}{3} = \frac{17}{12}$ **or** $1\frac{5}{12}$

2) $\frac{1}{2} + \frac{1}{2} = $ **1**

3) $\frac{1}{4} + \frac{1}{3} = \frac{7}{12}$

4) $\frac{1}{5} + \frac{1}{3} = \frac{8}{15}$

5) $\frac{1}{2} + \frac{3}{4} = \frac{5}{4}$ **or** $1\frac{1}{4}$

6) $\frac{1}{2} + \frac{1}{3} = \frac{5}{6}$

7) $\frac{1}{3} + \frac{1}{2} = \frac{5}{6}$

8) $\frac{1}{3} + \frac{2}{3} = $ **1**

9) $\frac{3}{4} + \frac{3}{4} = \frac{3}{2}$ **or** $1\frac{1}{2}$

10) $\frac{2}{5} + \frac{2}{3} = \frac{16}{15}$ **or** $1\frac{1}{15}$

11) $\frac{2}{3} + \frac{3}{4} = \frac{17}{12}$ **or** $1\frac{5}{12}$

12) $\frac{1}{2} + \frac{3}{5} = \frac{11}{10}$ **or** $1\frac{1}{10}$

13) $\frac{1}{2} + \frac{1}{2} = $ **1**

14) $\frac{4}{5} + \frac{1}{3} = \frac{17}{15}$ **or** $1\frac{2}{15}$

15) $\frac{1}{2} + \frac{2}{3} = \frac{7}{6}$ **or** $1\frac{1}{6}$

16) $\frac{2}{3} + \frac{1}{2} = \frac{7}{6}$ **or** $1\frac{1}{6}$

14/42

17) $\frac{1}{2} + \frac{1}{3} = \frac{5}{6}$

18) $\frac{2}{5} + \frac{1}{5} = \frac{3}{5}$

19) $\frac{1}{3} + \frac{1}{2} = \frac{5}{6}$

20) $\frac{1}{3} + \frac{3}{5} = \frac{14}{15}$

21) $\frac{1}{2} + \frac{1}{2} = $ **1**

22) $\frac{1}{3} + \frac{3}{4} = \frac{13}{12}$ **or** $1\frac{1}{12}$

23) $\frac{1}{2} + \frac{1}{2} = $ **1**

24) $\frac{1}{4} + \frac{2}{3} = \frac{11}{12}$

25) $\frac{1}{2} + \frac{1}{3} = \frac{5}{6}$

26) $\frac{1}{2} + \frac{2}{3} = \frac{7}{6}$ **or** $1\frac{1}{6}$

27) $\frac{4}{5} + \frac{1}{2} = \frac{13}{10}$ **or** $1\frac{3}{10}$

28) $\frac{2}{5} + \frac{1}{2} = \frac{9}{10}$

29) $\frac{4}{5} + \frac{2}{3} = \frac{22}{15}$ **or** $1\frac{7}{15}$

30) $\frac{1}{2} + \frac{1}{4} = \frac{3}{4}$

1) $\frac{1}{3} + \frac{1}{3} = \frac{2}{3}$

2) $\frac{2}{5} + \frac{3}{4} = \frac{23}{20}$ **or** $1\frac{3}{20}$

3) $\frac{2}{3} + \frac{3}{5} = \frac{19}{15}$ **or** $1\frac{4}{15}$

4) $\frac{2}{3} + \frac{1}{2} = \frac{7}{6}$ **or** $1\frac{1}{6}$

5) $\frac{2}{5} + \frac{1}{2} = \frac{9}{10}$

6) $\frac{2}{3} + 1 = \frac{5}{3}$ **or** $1\frac{2}{3}$

7) $\frac{1}{5} + \frac{1}{3} = \frac{8}{15}$

8) $\frac{4}{5} + \frac{1}{2} = \frac{13}{10}$ **or** $1\frac{3}{10}$

9) $\frac{2}{5} + \frac{3}{4} = \frac{23}{20}$ **or** $1\frac{3}{20}$

10) $\frac{1}{2} + \frac{1}{2} = \mathbf{1}$

11) $\frac{1}{2} + \frac{3}{5} = \frac{11}{10}$ **or** $1\frac{1}{10}$

12) $\frac{1}{4} + \frac{1}{4} = \frac{1}{2}$

13) $\frac{1}{2} + \frac{1}{2} = \mathbf{1}$

14) $\frac{1}{2} + \frac{4}{5} = \frac{13}{10}$ **or** $1\frac{3}{10}$

15) $\frac{1}{3} + \frac{1}{2} = \frac{5}{6}$

16) $\frac{1}{2} + \frac{1}{4} = \frac{3}{4}$

17) $\frac{1}{3} + \frac{1}{3} = \frac{2}{3}$

15/42

18) $\frac{4}{5} + \frac{3}{4} = \frac{31}{20}$ **or** $1\frac{11}{20}$

19) $\frac{1}{2} + \frac{1}{2} = \mathbf{1}$

20) $\frac{2}{3} + \frac{3}{4} = \frac{17}{12}$ **or** $1\frac{5}{12}$

21) $\frac{1}{3} + \frac{4}{5} = \frac{17}{15}$ **or** $1\frac{2}{15}$

22) $\frac{1}{2} + \frac{2}{3} = \frac{7}{6}$ **or** $1\frac{1}{6}$

23) $\frac{1}{2} + \frac{1}{3} = \frac{5}{6}$

24) $\frac{2}{3} + \frac{2}{3} = \frac{4}{3}$ **or** $1\frac{1}{3}$

25) $\frac{3}{4} + \frac{2}{5} = \frac{23}{20}$ **or** $1\frac{3}{20}$

26) $1 + \frac{3}{5} = \frac{8}{5}$ **or** $1\frac{3}{5}$

27) $\frac{1}{2} + \frac{1}{5} = \frac{7}{10}$

28) $\frac{2}{5} + \frac{1}{2} = \frac{9}{10}$

29) $\frac{1}{2} + \frac{4}{5} = \frac{13}{10}$ **or** $1\frac{3}{10}$

30) $\frac{4}{5} + \frac{1}{2} = \frac{13}{10}$ **or** $1\frac{3}{10}$

1) $\frac{7}{2} + \frac{33}{8} = \frac{61}{8}$ **or** $7\frac{5}{8}$

2) $\frac{19}{8} + \frac{7}{2} = \frac{47}{8}$ **or** $5\frac{7}{8}$

3) $4 + \frac{7}{4} = \frac{23}{4}$ **or** $5\frac{3}{4}$

4) $\frac{9}{2} + \frac{2}{5} = \frac{49}{10}$ **or** $4\frac{9}{10}$

5) $\frac{15}{7} + \frac{5}{3} = \frac{80}{21}$ **or** $3\frac{17}{21}$

6) $\frac{17}{5} + \frac{4}{5} = \frac{21}{5}$ **or** $4\frac{1}{5}$

7) $\frac{39}{8} + \frac{19}{5} = \frac{347}{40}$ **or** $8\frac{27}{40}$

8) $5 + \frac{19}{4} = \frac{39}{4}$ **or** $9\frac{3}{4}$

9) $\frac{17}{5} + \frac{1}{2} = \frac{39}{10}$ **or** $3\frac{9}{10}$

10) $3 + \frac{9}{8} = \frac{33}{8}$ **or** $4\frac{1}{8}$

11) $\frac{9}{4} + \frac{9}{4} = \frac{9}{2}$ **or** $4\frac{1}{2}$

12) $\frac{5}{2} + \frac{1}{3} = \frac{17}{6}$ **or** $2\frac{5}{6}$

13) $\frac{5}{2} + \frac{7}{3} = \frac{29}{6}$ **or** $4\frac{5}{6}$

14) $\frac{7}{5} + 3 = \frac{22}{5}$ **or** $4\frac{2}{5}$

15) $\frac{11}{6} + \frac{31}{8} = \frac{137}{24}$ **or** $5\frac{17}{24}$

16) $\frac{35}{8} + \frac{2}{3} = \frac{121}{24}$ **or** $5\frac{1}{24}$

17) $\frac{9}{2} + \frac{17}{8} = \frac{53}{8}$ **or** $6\frac{5}{8}$

16/42

18) $\frac{3}{7} + \frac{3}{2} = \frac{27}{14}$ **or** $1\frac{13}{14}$

19) $\frac{4}{3} + \frac{10}{3} = \frac{14}{3}$ **or** $4\frac{2}{3}$

20) $\frac{7}{3} + \frac{11}{5} = \frac{68}{15}$ **or** $4\frac{8}{15}$

21) $3 + \frac{3}{7} = \frac{24}{7}$ **or** $3\frac{3}{7}$

22) $\frac{12}{7} + \frac{6}{5} = \frac{102}{35}$ **or** $2\frac{32}{35}$

23) $\frac{3}{8} + \frac{12}{7} = \frac{117}{56}$ **or** $2\frac{5}{56}$

24) $1 + \frac{4}{3} = \frac{7}{3}$ **or** $2\frac{1}{3}$

25) $4 + \frac{13}{4} = \frac{29}{4}$ **or** $7\frac{1}{4}$

26) $\frac{29}{8} + \frac{9}{2} = \frac{65}{8}$ **or** $8\frac{1}{8}$

27) $\frac{9}{8} + \frac{21}{5} = \frac{213}{40}$ **or** $5\frac{13}{40}$

28) $\frac{17}{6} + 5 = \frac{47}{6}$ **or** $7\frac{5}{6}$

29) $3 + \frac{15}{7} = \frac{36}{7}$ **or** $5\frac{1}{7}$

30) $\frac{7}{3} + \frac{7}{2} = \frac{35}{6}$ **or** $5\frac{5}{6}$

1) $\frac{1}{8} + \frac{31}{7} = \frac{255}{56}$ **or** $4\frac{31}{56}$

2) $\frac{11}{3} + \frac{9}{2} = \frac{49}{6}$ **or** $8\frac{1}{6}$

3) $\frac{10}{7} + 3 = \frac{31}{7}$ **or** $4\frac{3}{7}$

4) $\frac{7}{2} + 4 = \frac{15}{2}$ **or** $7\frac{1}{2}$

5) $\frac{1}{7} + 1 = \frac{8}{7}$ **or** $1\frac{1}{7}$

6) $\frac{7}{3} + \frac{4}{3} = \frac{11}{3}$ **or** $3\frac{2}{3}$

7) $\frac{23}{5} + \frac{13}{5} = \frac{36}{5}$ **or** $7\frac{1}{5}$

8) $\frac{17}{4} + \frac{19}{4} = $ **9**

9) $\frac{5}{8} + \frac{7}{8} = \frac{3}{2}$ **or** $1\frac{1}{2}$

10) $\frac{5}{2} + \frac{13}{5} = \frac{51}{10}$ **or** $5\frac{1}{10}$

11) $5 + \frac{11}{8} = \frac{51}{8}$ **or** $6\frac{3}{8}$

12) $\frac{19}{5} + \frac{7}{2} = \frac{73}{10}$ **or** $7\frac{3}{10}$

13) $\frac{19}{6} + \frac{1}{3} = \frac{7}{2}$ **or** $3\frac{1}{2}$

14) $\frac{12}{7} + \frac{20}{7} = \frac{32}{7}$ **or** $4\frac{4}{7}$

15) $\frac{20}{7} + \frac{17}{8} = \frac{279}{56}$ **or** $4\frac{55}{56}$

16) $\frac{19}{4} + 2 = \frac{27}{4}$ **or** $6\frac{3}{4}$

17/42

17) $\frac{9}{2} + \frac{16}{3} = \frac{59}{6}$ **or** $9\frac{5}{6}$

18) $\frac{17}{7} + \frac{11}{5} = \frac{162}{35}$ **or** $4\frac{22}{35}$

19) $\frac{3}{5} + \frac{17}{4} = \frac{97}{20}$ **or** $4\frac{17}{20}$

20) $\frac{4}{3} + \frac{8}{7} = \frac{52}{21}$ **or** $2\frac{10}{21}$

21) $\frac{2}{3} + \frac{13}{4} = \frac{47}{12}$ **or** $3\frac{11}{12}$

22) $\frac{7}{2} + \frac{22}{7} = \frac{93}{14}$ **or** $6\frac{9}{14}$

23) $\frac{5}{2} + \frac{9}{2} = $ **7**

24) $\frac{29}{7} + 3 = \frac{50}{7}$ **or** $7\frac{1}{7}$

25) $\frac{13}{4} + \frac{1}{6} = \frac{41}{12}$ **or** $3\frac{5}{12}$

26) $\frac{4}{5} + \frac{14}{5} = \frac{18}{5}$ **or** $3\frac{3}{5}$

27) $\frac{12}{5} + \frac{23}{7} = \frac{199}{35}$ **or** $5\frac{24}{35}$

28) $\frac{2}{5} + \frac{3}{4} = \frac{23}{20}$ **or** $1\frac{3}{20}$

29) $\frac{22}{7} + 3 = \frac{43}{7}$ **or** $6\frac{1}{7}$

30) $\frac{23}{7} + \frac{30}{7} = \frac{53}{7}$ **or** $7\frac{4}{7}$

1) $\frac{1}{6} + \frac{39}{8} = \frac{121}{24}$ **or** $5\frac{1}{24}$

2) $\frac{14}{3} + \frac{5}{2} = \frac{43}{6}$ **or** $7\frac{1}{6}$

3) $\frac{5}{8} + \frac{3}{5} = \frac{49}{40}$ **or** $1\frac{9}{40}$

4) $5 + \frac{7}{2} = \frac{17}{2}$ **or** $8\frac{1}{2}$

5) $\frac{5}{8} + 5 = \frac{45}{8}$ **or** $5\frac{5}{8}$

6) $\frac{6}{5} + 4 = \frac{26}{5}$ **or** $5\frac{1}{5}$

7) $\frac{8}{7} + \frac{15}{4} = \frac{137}{28}$ **or** $4\frac{25}{28}$

8) $\frac{37}{8} + 5 = \frac{77}{8}$ **or** $9\frac{5}{8}$

9) $3 + \frac{4}{3} = \frac{13}{3}$ **or** $4\frac{1}{3}$

10) $4 + \frac{1}{3} = \frac{13}{3}$ **or** $4\frac{1}{3}$

11) $\frac{1}{3} + \frac{5}{2} = \frac{17}{6}$ **or** $2\frac{5}{6}$

12) $2 + \frac{13}{4} = \frac{21}{4}$ **or** $5\frac{1}{4}$

13) $\frac{9}{4} + \frac{5}{7} = \frac{83}{28}$ **or** $2\frac{27}{28}$

14) $1 + \frac{3}{4} = \frac{7}{4}$ **or** $1\frac{3}{4}$

15) $\frac{34}{7} + \frac{21}{5} = \frac{317}{35}$ **or** $9\frac{2}{35}$

16) $\frac{3}{2} + \frac{7}{2} = $ **5**

17) $\frac{31}{8} + \frac{11}{6} = \frac{137}{24}$ **or** $5\frac{17}{24}$

18/42

18) $\frac{24}{5} + \frac{5}{2} = \frac{73}{10}$ **or** $7\frac{3}{10}$

19) $\frac{9}{8} + \frac{3}{7} = \frac{87}{56}$ **or** $1\frac{31}{56}$

20) $\frac{5}{2} + \frac{14}{3} = \frac{43}{6}$ **or** $7\frac{1}{6}$

21) $\frac{7}{3} + 5 = \frac{22}{3}$ **or** $7\frac{1}{3}$

22) $\frac{5}{3} + 3 = \frac{14}{3}$ **or** $4\frac{2}{3}$

23) $2 + \frac{2}{3} = \frac{8}{3}$ **or** $2\frac{2}{3}$

24) $\frac{1}{2} + 4 = \frac{9}{2}$ **or** $4\frac{1}{2}$

25) $\frac{1}{3} + \frac{3}{2} = \frac{11}{6}$ **or** $1\frac{5}{6}$

26) $4 + \frac{25}{7} = \frac{53}{7}$ **or** $7\frac{4}{7}$

27) $4 + \frac{19}{4} = \frac{35}{4}$ **or** $8\frac{3}{4}$

28) $\frac{7}{2} + \frac{15}{4} = \frac{29}{4}$ **or** $7\frac{1}{4}$

29) $\frac{16}{7} + 3 = \frac{37}{7}$ **or** $5\frac{2}{7}$

30) $\frac{4}{7} + \frac{24}{5} = \frac{188}{35}$ **or** $5\frac{13}{35}$

1) $\frac{7}{2} + \frac{5}{4} = \frac{19}{4}$ **or** $4\frac{3}{4}$

2) $5 + \frac{22}{5} = \frac{47}{5}$ **or** $9\frac{2}{5}$

3) $\frac{5}{2} + \frac{6}{5} = \frac{37}{10}$ **or** $3\frac{7}{10}$

4) $\frac{3}{2} + \frac{1}{2} =$ **2**

5) $\frac{35}{8} + \frac{3}{4} = \frac{41}{8}$ **or** $5\frac{1}{8}$

6) $\frac{9}{4} + 5 = \frac{29}{4}$ **or** $7\frac{1}{4}$

7) $3 + \frac{30}{7} = \frac{51}{7}$ **or** $7\frac{2}{7}$

8) $4 + \frac{1}{2} = \frac{9}{2}$ **or** $4\frac{1}{2}$

9) $\frac{1}{7} + 2 = \frac{15}{7}$ **or** $2\frac{1}{7}$

10) $\frac{11}{5} + \frac{10}{3} = \frac{83}{15}$ **or** $5\frac{8}{15}$

11) $\frac{16}{7} + \frac{9}{2} = \frac{95}{14}$ **or** $6\frac{11}{14}$

12) $\frac{3}{2} + \frac{9}{2} =$ **6**

13) $5 + \frac{4}{5} = \frac{29}{5}$ **or** $5\frac{4}{5}$

14) $\frac{25}{8} + \frac{23}{7} = \frac{359}{56}$ **or** $6\frac{23}{56}$

15) $\frac{21}{8} + \frac{9}{2} = \frac{57}{8}$ **or** $7\frac{1}{8}$

16) $5 + \frac{5}{6} = \frac{35}{6}$ **or** $5\frac{5}{6}$

17) $\frac{3}{2} + \frac{3}{5} = \frac{21}{10}$ **or** $2\frac{1}{10}$

18) $\frac{16}{5} + \frac{5}{3} = \frac{73}{15}$ **or** $4\frac{13}{15}$

19) $\frac{16}{5} + 1 = \frac{21}{5}$ **or** $4\frac{1}{5}$

20) $\frac{5}{3} + \frac{1}{2} = \frac{13}{6}$ **or** $2\frac{1}{6}$

21) $\frac{32}{7} + 2 = \frac{46}{7}$ **or** $6\frac{4}{7}$

22) $\frac{21}{5} + 3 = \frac{36}{5}$ **or** $7\frac{1}{5}$

23) $\frac{3}{2} + \frac{19}{4} = \frac{25}{4}$ **or** $6\frac{1}{4}$

24) $\frac{10}{3} + 3 = \frac{19}{3}$ **or** $6\frac{1}{3}$

25) $\frac{9}{2} + 4 = \frac{17}{2}$ **or** $8\frac{1}{2}$

26) $3 + \frac{9}{8} = \frac{33}{8}$ **or** $4\frac{1}{8}$

27) $\frac{7}{2} + 1 = \frac{9}{2}$ **or** $4\frac{1}{2}$

28) $5 + \frac{7}{2} = \frac{17}{2}$ **or** $8\frac{1}{2}$

29) $\frac{15}{4} + \frac{1}{2} = \frac{17}{4}$ **or** $4\frac{1}{4}$

30) $\frac{26}{7} + 2 = \frac{40}{7}$ **or** $5\frac{5}{7}$

19/42

1) $\frac{17}{8} + 2 = \frac{33}{8}$ **or** $4\frac{1}{8}$

2) $\frac{7}{2} + \frac{11}{8} = \frac{39}{8}$ **or** $4\frac{7}{8}$

3) $\frac{3}{2} + \frac{7}{2} = $ **5**

4) $\frac{8}{3} + \frac{1}{3} = $ **3**

5) $5 + \frac{4}{3} = \frac{19}{3}$ **or** $6\frac{1}{3}$

6) $\frac{23}{8} + \frac{3}{2} = \frac{35}{8}$ **or** $4\frac{3}{8}$

7) $\frac{19}{4} + \frac{21}{5} = \frac{179}{20}$ **or** $8\frac{19}{20}$

8) $\frac{5}{3} + \frac{5}{2} = \frac{25}{6}$ **or** $4\frac{1}{6}$

9) $\frac{1}{8} + \frac{13}{5} = \frac{109}{40}$ **or** $2\frac{29}{40}$

10) $5 + \frac{1}{2} = \frac{11}{2}$ **or** $5\frac{1}{2}$

11) $\frac{22}{7} + \frac{6}{7} = $ **4**

12) $\frac{5}{4} + 2 = \frac{13}{4}$ **or** $3\frac{1}{4}$

13) $\frac{2}{3} + \frac{7}{4} = \frac{29}{12}$ **or** $2\frac{5}{12}$

14) $\frac{7}{3} + 4 = \frac{19}{3}$ **or** $6\frac{1}{3}$

15) $\frac{7}{2} + \frac{9}{5} = \frac{53}{10}$ **or** $5\frac{3}{10}$

16) $\frac{7}{2} + \frac{21}{5} = \frac{77}{10}$ **or** $7\frac{7}{10}$

17) $\frac{5}{2} + 3 = \frac{11}{2}$ **or** $5\frac{1}{2}$

20/42

18) $\frac{15}{7} + \frac{3}{2} = \frac{51}{14}$ **or** $3\frac{9}{14}$

19) $\frac{29}{7} + \frac{29}{7} = \frac{58}{7}$ **or** $8\frac{2}{7}$

20) $\frac{30}{7} + 5 = \frac{65}{7}$ **or** $9\frac{2}{7}$

21) $\frac{4}{7} + 1 = \frac{11}{7}$ **or** $1\frac{4}{7}$

22) $\frac{1}{6} + \frac{30}{7} = \frac{187}{42}$ **or** $4\frac{19}{42}$

23) $\frac{33}{7} + \frac{9}{7} = $ **6**

24) $\frac{18}{5} + \frac{35}{8} = \frac{319}{40}$ **or** $7\frac{39}{40}$

25) $\frac{9}{7} + \frac{8}{3} = \frac{83}{21}$ **or** $3\frac{20}{21}$

26) $\frac{12}{5} + \frac{7}{3} = \frac{71}{15}$ **or** $4\frac{11}{15}$

27) $\frac{5}{6} + \frac{1}{4} = \frac{13}{12}$ **or** $1\frac{1}{12}$

28) $5 + \frac{15}{4} = \frac{35}{4}$ **or** $8\frac{3}{4}$

29) $5 + \frac{11}{4} = \frac{31}{4}$ **or** $7\frac{3}{4}$

30) $3 + \frac{19}{5} = \frac{34}{5}$ **or** $6\frac{4}{5}$

1) $\frac{3}{4} - \frac{1}{2} = \frac{1}{4}$

2) $\frac{2}{3} - \frac{1}{2} = \frac{1}{6}$

3) $\frac{3}{5} - \frac{1}{2} = \frac{1}{10}$

4) $\frac{3}{4} - \frac{1}{2} = \frac{1}{4}$

5) $\frac{3}{5} - \frac{2}{5} = \frac{1}{5}$

6) $\frac{1}{3} - \frac{1}{4} = \frac{1}{12}$

7) $\frac{1}{2} - \frac{2}{5} = \frac{1}{10}$

8) $\frac{3}{5} - \frac{1}{2} = \frac{1}{10}$

9) $\frac{2}{5} - \frac{1}{3} = \frac{1}{15}$

10) $\frac{1}{4} - \frac{1}{4} = \mathbf{0}$

11) $\frac{1}{2} - \frac{1}{5} = \frac{3}{10}$

12) $\frac{1}{2} - \frac{2}{5} = \frac{1}{10}$

13) $\frac{1}{2} - \frac{1}{2} = \mathbf{0}$

14) $\frac{3}{5} - \frac{1}{3} = \frac{4}{15}$

15) $\frac{1}{2} - \frac{1}{4} = \frac{1}{4}$

16) $\frac{2}{3} - \frac{1}{5} = \frac{7}{15}$

17) $\frac{1}{2} - \frac{1}{2} = \mathbf{0}$

18) $\frac{1}{3} - \frac{1}{5} = \frac{2}{15}$

19) $1 - \frac{3}{4} = \frac{1}{4}$

20) $\frac{1}{2} - \frac{1}{4} = \frac{1}{4}$

21) $\frac{3}{4} - \frac{1}{5} = \frac{11}{20}$

22) $\frac{4}{5} - \frac{3}{4} = \frac{1}{20}$

23) $1 - \frac{3}{5} = \frac{2}{5}$

24) $\frac{1}{2} - \frac{1}{4} = \frac{1}{4}$

25) $\frac{4}{5} - \frac{2}{3} = \frac{2}{15}$

26) $\frac{1}{2} - \frac{1}{2} = \mathbf{0}$

27) $\frac{2}{3} - \frac{1}{3} = \frac{1}{3}$

28) $\frac{3}{4} - \frac{1}{4} = \frac{1}{2}$

29) $\frac{2}{3} - \frac{1}{3} = \frac{1}{3}$

30) $\frac{1}{2} - \frac{1}{5} = \frac{3}{10}$

1) $\frac{1}{2} - \frac{1}{3} = \frac{1}{6}$

2) $1 - \frac{1}{2} = \frac{1}{2}$

3) $\frac{3}{5} - \frac{1}{2} = \frac{1}{10}$

4) $\frac{2}{3} - \frac{1}{2} = \frac{1}{6}$

5) $\frac{4}{5} - \frac{1}{5} = \frac{3}{5}$

6) $\frac{3}{4} - \frac{2}{5} = \frac{7}{20}$

7) $\frac{1}{3} - \frac{1}{4} = \frac{1}{12}$

8) $\frac{1}{2} - \frac{1}{5} = \frac{3}{10}$

9) $\frac{4}{5} - \frac{1}{2} = \frac{3}{10}$

10) $\frac{3}{4} - \frac{1}{2} = \frac{1}{4}$

11) $\frac{4}{5} - \frac{1}{3} = \frac{7}{15}$

12) $\frac{3}{4} - \frac{1}{3} = \frac{5}{12}$

13) $\frac{1}{2} - \frac{1}{4} = \frac{1}{4}$

14) $\frac{2}{3} - \frac{1}{2} = \frac{1}{6}$

15) $\frac{1}{2} - \frac{1}{4} = \frac{1}{4}$

16) $\frac{1}{4} - \frac{1}{5} = \frac{1}{20}$

17) $\frac{4}{5} - \frac{1}{2} = \frac{3}{10}$

18) $\frac{2}{3} - \frac{1}{5} = \frac{7}{15}$

19) $\frac{1}{2} - \frac{1}{4} = \frac{1}{4}$

20) $\frac{2}{5} - \frac{1}{4} = \frac{3}{20}$

21) $\frac{4}{5} - \frac{1}{2} = \frac{3}{10}$

22) $\frac{3}{5} - \frac{1}{2} = \frac{1}{10}$

23) $\frac{2}{3} - \frac{1}{3} = \frac{1}{3}$

24) $\frac{3}{5} - \frac{1}{4} = \frac{7}{20}$

25) $\frac{4}{5} - \frac{1}{2} = \frac{3}{10}$

26) $\frac{3}{5} - \frac{1}{5} = \frac{2}{5}$

27) $\frac{3}{5} - \frac{2}{5} = \frac{1}{5}$

28) $\frac{3}{4} - \frac{1}{2} = \frac{1}{4}$

29) $1 - \frac{2}{5} = \frac{3}{5}$

30) $\frac{1}{2} - \frac{1}{2} = \mathbf{0}$

22/42

1) $\frac{1}{4} - \frac{1}{4} =$ **0**

2) $\frac{1}{2} - \frac{1}{4} = \frac{1}{4}$

3) $\frac{2}{3} - \frac{1}{2} = \frac{1}{6}$

4) $\frac{1}{2} - \frac{1}{5} = \frac{3}{10}$

5) $\frac{3}{4} - \frac{1}{2} = \frac{1}{4}$

6) $\frac{2}{3} - \frac{1}{3} = \frac{1}{3}$

7) $\frac{4}{5} - \frac{1}{2} = \frac{3}{10}$

8) $\frac{1}{2} - \frac{1}{3} = \frac{1}{6}$

9) $\frac{3}{4} - \frac{2}{3} = \frac{1}{12}$

10) $\frac{1}{2} - \frac{1}{2} =$ **0**

11) $\frac{3}{4} - \frac{1}{3} = \frac{5}{12}$

12) $1 - \frac{1}{4} = \frac{3}{4}$

13) $\frac{1}{2} - \frac{1}{3} = \frac{1}{6}$

14) $\frac{2}{5} - \frac{1}{3} = \frac{1}{15}$

15) $\frac{4}{5} - \frac{1}{5} = \frac{3}{5}$

16) $\frac{2}{3} - \frac{2}{5} = \frac{4}{15}$

17) $\frac{2}{3} - \frac{1}{2} = \frac{1}{6}$

18) $\frac{4}{5} - \frac{1}{2} = \frac{3}{10}$

19) $\frac{3}{4} - \frac{1}{3} = \frac{5}{12}$

20) $\frac{1}{2} - \frac{1}{3} = \frac{1}{6}$

21) $\frac{3}{4} - \frac{1}{2} = \frac{1}{4}$

22) $\frac{2}{3} - \frac{1}{3} = \frac{1}{3}$

23) $\frac{1}{2} - \frac{2}{5} = \frac{1}{10}$

24) $\frac{3}{4} - \frac{1}{2} = \frac{1}{4}$

25) $\frac{2}{3} - \frac{1}{3} = \frac{1}{3}$

26) $\frac{1}{2} - \frac{1}{4} = \frac{1}{4}$

27) $\frac{2}{3} - \frac{1}{3} = \frac{1}{3}$

28) $\frac{4}{5} - \frac{3}{5} = \frac{1}{5}$

29) $\frac{1}{2} - \frac{2}{5} = \frac{1}{10}$

30) $\frac{3}{4} - \frac{1}{2} = \frac{1}{4}$

23/42

1) $\frac{3}{4} - \frac{2}{3} = \frac{1}{12}$

2) $\frac{3}{4} - \frac{1}{2} = \frac{1}{4}$

3) $\frac{4}{5} - \frac{1}{2} = \frac{3}{10}$

4) $1 - \frac{3}{5} = \frac{2}{5}$

5) $\frac{2}{3} - \frac{1}{2} = \frac{1}{6}$

6) $\frac{3}{5} - \frac{1}{2} = \frac{1}{10}$

7) $\frac{3}{4} - \frac{1}{5} = \frac{11}{20}$

8) $\frac{1}{2} - \frac{1}{2} = 0$

9) $\frac{3}{4} - \frac{1}{2} = \frac{1}{4}$

10) $\frac{4}{5} - \frac{2}{3} = \frac{2}{15}$

11) $\frac{3}{5} - \frac{1}{2} = \frac{1}{10}$

12) $\frac{1}{2} - \frac{1}{4} = \frac{1}{4}$

13) $\frac{2}{3} - \frac{2}{5} = \frac{4}{15}$

14) $\frac{3}{4} - \frac{1}{5} = \frac{11}{20}$

15) $\frac{4}{5} - \frac{1}{5} = \frac{3}{5}$

16) $\frac{2}{3} - \frac{1}{2} = \frac{1}{6}$

17) $\frac{2}{3} - \frac{2}{3} = 0$

18) $\frac{3}{5} - \frac{1}{3} = \frac{4}{15}$

19) $\frac{1}{2} - \frac{2}{5} = \frac{1}{10}$

20) $\frac{4}{5} - \frac{3}{5} = \frac{1}{5}$

21) $\frac{4}{5} - \frac{1}{2} = \frac{3}{10}$

22) $\frac{2}{5} - \frac{1}{3} = \frac{1}{15}$

23) $\frac{2}{3} - \frac{1}{2} = \frac{1}{6}$

24) $\frac{2}{3} - \frac{2}{5} = \frac{4}{15}$

25) $\frac{2}{3} - \frac{1}{2} = \frac{1}{6}$

26) $\frac{3}{4} - \frac{1}{2} = \frac{1}{4}$

27) $\frac{1}{2} - \frac{2}{5} = \frac{1}{10}$

28) $\frac{1}{3} - \frac{1}{3} = 0$

29) $\frac{2}{3} - \frac{1}{2} = \frac{1}{6}$

30) $\frac{4}{5} - \frac{2}{3} = \frac{2}{15}$

1) $\frac{1}{2} - \frac{1}{3} = \frac{1}{6}$

2) $\frac{2}{5} - \frac{1}{4} = \frac{3}{20}$

3) $\frac{1}{2} - \frac{1}{2} = 0$

4) $\frac{3}{4} - \frac{1}{2} = \frac{1}{4}$

5) $\frac{4}{5} - \frac{4}{5} = 0$

6) $\frac{4}{5} - \frac{1}{4} = \frac{11}{20}$

7) $\frac{1}{3} - \frac{1}{3} = 0$

8) $\frac{4}{5} - \frac{1}{2} = \frac{3}{10}$

9) $\frac{1}{2} - \frac{1}{2} = 0$

10) $\frac{3}{4} - \frac{1}{5} = \frac{11}{20}$

11) $\frac{1}{2} - \frac{1}{5} = \frac{3}{10}$

12) $\frac{3}{4} - \frac{2}{5} = \frac{7}{20}$

13) $\frac{1}{3} - \frac{1}{3} = 0$

14) $\frac{3}{4} - \frac{3}{5} = \frac{3}{20}$

15) $\frac{1}{2} - \frac{2}{5} = \frac{1}{10}$

16) $\frac{1}{2} - \frac{1}{5} = \frac{3}{10}$

17) $\frac{3}{4} - \frac{1}{2} = \frac{1}{4}$

18) $\frac{2}{3} - \frac{1}{2} = \frac{1}{6}$

19) $\frac{1}{2} - \frac{1}{5} = \frac{3}{10}$

20) $\frac{2}{3} - \frac{1}{2} = \frac{1}{6}$

21) $\frac{4}{5} - \frac{1}{2} = \frac{3}{10}$

22) $\frac{2}{5} - \frac{1}{4} = \frac{3}{20}$

23) $\frac{1}{2} - \frac{1}{5} = \frac{3}{10}$

24) $\frac{3}{4} - \frac{1}{2} = \frac{1}{4}$

25) $\frac{1}{2} - \frac{2}{5} = \frac{1}{10}$

26) $\frac{4}{5} - \frac{1}{5} = \frac{3}{5}$

27) $\frac{2}{5} - \frac{1}{3} = \frac{1}{15}$

28) $\frac{3}{4} - \frac{1}{3} = \frac{5}{12}$

29) $\frac{2}{3} - \frac{1}{2} = \frac{1}{6}$

30) $\frac{1}{2} - \frac{1}{2} = 0$

25/42

1) $\frac{23}{6} - 2 = \frac{11}{6}$ **or** $1\frac{5}{6}$

2) $\frac{10}{3} - \frac{6}{5} = \frac{32}{15}$ **or** $2\frac{2}{15}$

3) $\frac{24}{5} - \frac{17}{6} = \frac{59}{30}$ **or** $1\frac{29}{30}$

4) $2 - \frac{4}{3} = \frac{2}{3}$

5) $\frac{9}{2} - \frac{25}{8} = \frac{11}{8}$ **or** $1\frac{3}{8}$

6) $\frac{22}{7} - \frac{4}{3} = \frac{38}{21}$ **or** $1\frac{17}{21}$

7) $\frac{7}{2} - \frac{27}{8} = \frac{1}{8}$

8) $\frac{14}{3} - \frac{13}{5} = \frac{31}{15}$ **or** $2\frac{1}{15}$

9) $\frac{23}{6} - \frac{1}{8} = \frac{89}{24}$ **or** $3\frac{17}{24}$

10) $\frac{12}{5} - \frac{1}{3} = \frac{31}{15}$ **or** $2\frac{1}{15}$

11) $\frac{17}{4} - \frac{5}{2} = \frac{7}{4}$ **or** $1\frac{3}{4}$

12) $\frac{9}{2} - \frac{6}{5} = \frac{33}{10}$ **or** $3\frac{3}{10}$

13) $\frac{14}{3} - \frac{1}{3} = \frac{13}{3}$ **or** $4\frac{1}{3}$

14) $\frac{15}{8} - 1 = \frac{7}{8}$

15) $5 - \frac{26}{7} = \frac{9}{7}$ **or** $1\frac{2}{7}$

16) $\frac{13}{4} - 1 = \frac{9}{4}$ **or** $2\frac{1}{4}$

17) $\frac{3}{2} - \frac{7}{6} = \frac{1}{3}$

26/42

18) $3 - \frac{13}{6} = \frac{5}{6}$

19) $\frac{34}{7} - 2 = \frac{20}{7}$ **or** $2\frac{6}{7}$

20) $2 - \frac{1}{4} = \frac{7}{4}$ **or** $1\frac{3}{4}$

21) $\frac{7}{2} - 1 = \frac{5}{2}$ **or** $2\frac{1}{2}$

22) $\frac{39}{8} - \frac{1}{2} = \frac{35}{8}$ **or** $4\frac{3}{8}$

23) $\frac{5}{3} - 1 = \frac{2}{3}$

24) $\frac{15}{4} - \frac{11}{6} = \frac{23}{12}$ **or** $1\frac{11}{12}$

25) $\frac{1}{4} - \frac{1}{7} = \frac{3}{28}$

26) $\frac{25}{8} - \frac{11}{5} = \frac{37}{40}$

27) $2 - \frac{2}{5} = \frac{8}{5}$ **or** $1\frac{3}{5}$

28) $3 - \frac{7}{3} = \frac{2}{3}$

29) $\frac{5}{3} - \frac{9}{7} = \frac{8}{21}$

30) $3 - \frac{7}{3} = \frac{2}{3}$

1) $\frac{11}{4} - \frac{17}{7} = \frac{9}{28}$

2) $\frac{17}{4} - 4 = \frac{1}{4}$

3) $\frac{23}{6} - \frac{7}{2} = \frac{1}{3}$

4) $5 - \frac{5}{3} = \frac{10}{3}$ **or** $3\frac{1}{3}$

5) $\frac{30}{7} - \frac{1}{2} = \frac{53}{14}$ **or** $3\frac{11}{14}$

6) $3 - \frac{11}{4} = \frac{1}{4}$

7) $\frac{13}{6} - \frac{1}{8} = \frac{49}{24}$ **or** $2\frac{1}{24}$

8) $\frac{17}{5} - \frac{5}{2} = \frac{9}{10}$

9) $5 - \frac{17}{5} = \frac{8}{5}$ **or** $1\frac{3}{5}$

10) $\frac{14}{3} - \frac{5}{7} = \frac{83}{21}$ **or** $3\frac{20}{21}$

11) $\frac{25}{6} - \frac{4}{3} = \frac{17}{6}$ **or** $2\frac{5}{6}$

12) $5 - \frac{7}{5} = \frac{18}{5}$ **or** $3\frac{3}{5}$

13) $\frac{15}{4} - \frac{26}{7} = \frac{1}{28}$

14) $\frac{13}{3} - 3 = \frac{4}{3}$ **or** $1\frac{1}{3}$

15) $\frac{7}{4} - \frac{4}{7} = \frac{33}{28}$ **or** $1\frac{5}{28}$

16) $\frac{15}{4} - \frac{7}{3} = \frac{17}{12}$ **or** $1\frac{5}{12}$

17) $\frac{11}{3} - 2 = \frac{5}{3}$ **or** $1\frac{2}{3}$

18) $\frac{5}{2} - \frac{5}{3} = \frac{5}{6}$

19) $\frac{7}{4} - 1 = \frac{3}{4}$

20) $3 - \frac{5}{2} = \frac{1}{2}$

21) $\frac{34}{7} - \frac{1}{8} = \frac{265}{56}$ **or** $4\frac{41}{56}$

22) $\frac{26}{7} - \frac{19}{6} = \frac{23}{42}$

23) $\frac{14}{3} - \frac{9}{2} = \frac{1}{6}$

24) $2 - \frac{3}{2} = \frac{1}{2}$

25) $4 - \frac{13}{6} = \frac{11}{6}$ **or** $1\frac{5}{6}$

26) $\frac{31}{7} - \frac{11}{5} = \frac{78}{35}$ **or** $2\frac{8}{35}$

27) $\frac{15}{4} - \frac{16}{7} = \frac{41}{28}$ **or** $1\frac{13}{28}$

28) $\frac{11}{8} - \frac{3}{5} = \frac{31}{40}$

29) $\frac{9}{2} - \frac{5}{3} = \frac{17}{6}$ **or** $2\frac{5}{6}$

30) $\frac{13}{6} - \frac{6}{5} = \frac{29}{30}$

27/42

1) $\frac{32}{7} - 1 = \frac{25}{7}$ **or** $3\frac{4}{7}$

2) $\frac{3}{2} - \frac{5}{4} = \frac{1}{4}$

3) $\frac{5}{2} - \frac{1}{2} =$ **2**

4) $4 - \frac{3}{2} = \frac{5}{2}$ **or** $2\frac{1}{2}$

5) $\frac{14}{3} - \frac{11}{8} = \frac{79}{24}$ **or** $3\frac{7}{24}$

6) $\frac{11}{7} - \frac{11}{8} = \frac{11}{56}$

7) $\frac{29}{8} - \frac{1}{4} = \frac{27}{8}$ **or** $3\frac{3}{8}$

8) $4 - \frac{14}{5} = \frac{6}{5}$ **or** $1\frac{1}{5}$

9) $3 - \frac{7}{8} = \frac{17}{8}$ **or** $2\frac{1}{8}$

10) $\frac{17}{4} - \frac{25}{6} = \frac{1}{12}$

11) $\frac{13}{3} - \frac{5}{3} = \frac{8}{3}$ **or** $2\frac{2}{3}$

12) $\frac{5}{2} - \frac{7}{8} = \frac{13}{8}$ **or** $1\frac{5}{8}$

13) $\frac{5}{3} - \frac{1}{2} = \frac{7}{6}$ **or** $1\frac{1}{6}$

14) $\frac{13}{4} - \frac{1}{2} = \frac{11}{4}$ **or** $2\frac{3}{4}$

15) $\frac{13}{3} - \frac{1}{5} = \frac{62}{15}$ **or** $4\frac{2}{15}$

16) $\frac{30}{7} - \frac{1}{2} = \frac{53}{14}$ **or** $3\frac{11}{14}$

17) $\frac{7}{5} - \frac{1}{5} = \frac{6}{5}$ **or** $1\frac{1}{5}$

28/42

18) $\frac{11}{5} - \frac{1}{6} = \frac{61}{30}$ **or** $2\frac{1}{30}$

19) $\frac{10}{3} - \frac{1}{2} = \frac{17}{6}$ **or** $2\frac{5}{6}$

20) $\frac{10}{3} - \frac{4}{3} =$ **2**

21) $3 - \frac{3}{4} = \frac{9}{4}$ **or** $2\frac{1}{4}$

22) $\frac{11}{4} - 2 = \frac{3}{4}$

23) $\frac{14}{3} - 2 = \frac{8}{3}$ **or** $2\frac{2}{3}$

24) $\frac{26}{7} - \frac{11}{3} = \frac{1}{21}$

25) $\frac{8}{3} - \frac{13}{8} = \frac{25}{24}$ **or** $1\frac{1}{24}$

26) $5 - \frac{7}{5} = \frac{18}{5}$ **or** $3\frac{3}{5}$

27) $\frac{7}{3} - 2 = \frac{1}{3}$

28) $5 - \frac{23}{8} = \frac{17}{8}$ **or** $2\frac{1}{8}$

29) $\frac{5}{2} - \frac{13}{7} = \frac{9}{14}$

30) $3 - \frac{3}{4} = \frac{9}{4}$ **or** $2\frac{1}{4}$

1) $\frac{29}{6} - 2 = \frac{17}{6}$ **or** $2\frac{5}{6}$

2) $\frac{31}{8} - \frac{11}{6} = \frac{49}{24}$ **or** $2\frac{1}{24}$

3) $\frac{21}{5} - \frac{17}{8} = \frac{83}{40}$ **or** $2\frac{3}{40}$

4) $\frac{25}{7} - \frac{13}{5} = \frac{34}{35}$

5) $\frac{19}{4} - \frac{11}{3} = \frac{13}{12}$ **or** $1\frac{1}{12}$

6) $\frac{14}{3} - \frac{31}{8} = \frac{19}{24}$

7) $\frac{21}{5} - \frac{9}{4} = \frac{39}{20}$ **or** $1\frac{19}{20}$

8) $\frac{27}{8} - \frac{17}{8} = \frac{5}{4}$ **or** $1\frac{1}{4}$

9) $\frac{5}{2} - \frac{9}{4} = \frac{1}{4}$

10) $\frac{30}{7} - \frac{8}{3} = \frac{34}{21}$ **or** $1\frac{13}{21}$

11) $\frac{31}{7} - \frac{19}{8} = \frac{115}{56}$ **or** $2\frac{3}{56}$

12) $\frac{21}{5} - \frac{5}{2} = \frac{17}{10}$ **or** $1\frac{7}{10}$

13) $3 - \frac{15}{7} = \frac{6}{7}$

14) $\frac{21}{5} - 2 = \frac{11}{5}$ **or** $2\frac{1}{5}$

15) $\frac{13}{6} - \frac{7}{4} = \frac{5}{12}$

16) $4 - \frac{7}{2} = \frac{1}{2}$

17) $\frac{5}{3} - \frac{1}{3} = \frac{4}{3}$ **or** $1\frac{1}{3}$

18) $\frac{15}{4} - \frac{6}{7} = \frac{81}{28}$ **or** $2\frac{25}{28}$

19) $\frac{13}{3} - \frac{3}{2} = \frac{17}{6}$ **or** $2\frac{5}{6}$

20) $\frac{10}{3} - \frac{2}{3} = \frac{8}{3}$ **or** $2\frac{2}{3}$

21) $\frac{35}{8} - \frac{18}{7} = \frac{101}{56}$ **or** $1\frac{45}{56}$

22) $\frac{7}{4} - \frac{13}{8} = \frac{1}{8}$

23) $3 - \frac{19}{7} = \frac{2}{7}$

24) $2 - \frac{1}{2} = \frac{3}{2}$ **or** $1\frac{1}{2}$

25) $\frac{23}{8} - \frac{2}{5} = \frac{99}{40}$ **or** $2\frac{19}{40}$

26) $5 - \frac{16}{5} = \frac{9}{5}$ **or** $1\frac{4}{5}$

27) $4 - \frac{18}{5} = \frac{2}{5}$

28) $\frac{9}{2} - \frac{7}{2} = \mathbf{1}$

29) $\frac{2}{3} - \frac{5}{8} = \frac{1}{24}$

30) $\frac{5}{3} - \frac{3}{2} = \frac{1}{6}$

29/42

1) $\frac{26}{5} - \frac{31}{6} = \frac{1}{30}$

2) $\frac{7}{2} - \frac{1}{3} = \frac{19}{6}$ **or** $3\frac{1}{6}$

3) $\frac{9}{4} - \frac{1}{2} = \frac{7}{4}$ **or** $1\frac{3}{4}$

4) $\frac{9}{2} - 4 = \frac{1}{2}$

5) $5 - \frac{29}{7} = \frac{6}{7}$

6) $\frac{11}{4} - \frac{5}{3} = \frac{13}{12}$ **or** $1\frac{1}{12}$

7) $\frac{7}{2} - 3 = \frac{1}{2}$

8) $\frac{19}{4} - \frac{5}{3} = \frac{37}{12}$ **or** $3\frac{1}{12}$

9) $\frac{1}{2} - \frac{2}{5} = \frac{1}{10}$

10) $\frac{11}{2} - \frac{9}{2} = \mathbf{1}$

11) $\frac{32}{7} - \frac{9}{5} = \frac{97}{35}$ **or** $2\frac{27}{35}$

12) $\frac{9}{2} - 1 = \frac{7}{2}$ **or** $3\frac{1}{2}$

13) $\frac{7}{2} - \frac{5}{4} = \frac{9}{4}$ **or** $2\frac{1}{4}$

14) $\frac{8}{3} - \frac{3}{2} = \frac{7}{6}$ **or** $1\frac{1}{6}$

15) $5 - \frac{21}{8} = \frac{19}{8}$ **or** $2\frac{3}{8}$

16) $\frac{23}{5} - \frac{7}{3} = \frac{34}{15}$ **or** $2\frac{4}{15}$

17) $\frac{11}{3} - \frac{1}{4} = \frac{41}{12}$ **or** $3\frac{5}{12}$

30/42

18) $\frac{18}{7} - \frac{7}{3} = \frac{5}{21}$

19) $\frac{14}{3} - \frac{9}{2} = \frac{1}{6}$

20) $\frac{22}{5} - 3 = \frac{7}{5}$ **or** $1\frac{2}{5}$

21) $3 - \frac{2}{5} = \frac{13}{5}$ **or** $2\frac{3}{5}$

22) $\frac{17}{4} - \frac{10}{3} = \frac{11}{12}$

23) $\frac{3}{2} - 1 = \frac{1}{2}$

24) $\frac{9}{2} - \frac{12}{7} = \frac{39}{14}$ **or** $2\frac{11}{14}$

25) $3 - \frac{1}{4} = \frac{11}{4}$ **or** $2\frac{3}{4}$

26) $\frac{3}{2} - 1 = \frac{1}{2}$

27) $\frac{29}{7} - \frac{7}{5} = \frac{96}{35}$ **or** $2\frac{26}{35}$

28) $\frac{24}{7} - \frac{10}{3} = \frac{2}{21}$

29) $2 - \frac{7}{4} = \frac{1}{4}$

30) $\frac{5}{2} - \frac{3}{2} = \mathbf{1}$

1) $\frac{2}{3} + \frac{1}{2} = \frac{7}{6}$ **or** $1\frac{1}{6}$

2) $\frac{3}{4} - \frac{1}{4} = \frac{1}{2}$

3) $\frac{1}{2} - \frac{1}{3} = \frac{1}{6}$

4) $\frac{1}{3} + \frac{1}{4} = \frac{7}{12}$

5) $\frac{1}{2} + \frac{1}{2} = \mathbf{1}$

6) $\frac{2}{3} - \frac{3}{5} = \frac{1}{15}$

7) $\frac{1}{2} + \frac{1}{2} = \mathbf{1}$

8) $1 - \frac{1}{5} = \frac{4}{5}$

9) $\frac{2}{3} + \frac{2}{5} = \frac{16}{15}$ **or** $1\frac{1}{15}$

10) $\frac{4}{5} + \frac{1}{2} = \frac{13}{10}$ **or** $1\frac{3}{10}$

11) $\frac{2}{3} - \frac{1}{2} = \frac{1}{6}$

12) $\frac{4}{5} - \frac{1}{3} = \frac{7}{15}$

13) $\frac{4}{5} - \frac{2}{5} = \frac{2}{5}$

14) $\frac{1}{5} + \frac{1}{3} = \frac{8}{15}$

15) $\frac{1}{2} - \frac{2}{5} = \frac{1}{10}$

16) $\frac{1}{3} + \frac{1}{2} = \frac{5}{6}$

17) $\frac{1}{2} + \frac{1}{2} = \mathbf{1}$

31/42

18) $\frac{3}{4} + \frac{1}{3} = \frac{13}{12}$ **or** $1\frac{1}{12}$

19) $\frac{1}{2} - \frac{1}{3} = \frac{1}{6}$

20) $\frac{1}{4} - \frac{1}{4} = \mathbf{0}$

21) $\frac{3}{4} - \frac{3}{5} = \frac{3}{20}$

22) $\frac{3}{5} + \frac{1}{2} = \frac{11}{10}$ **or** $1\frac{1}{10}$

23) $\frac{3}{4} - \frac{1}{4} = \frac{1}{2}$

24) $\frac{1}{2} + \frac{1}{2} = \mathbf{1}$

25) $\frac{2}{5} - \frac{1}{4} = \frac{3}{20}$

26) $\frac{3}{4} + \frac{1}{2} = \frac{5}{4}$ **or** $1\frac{1}{4}$

27) $\frac{2}{3} - \frac{2}{3} = \mathbf{0}$

28) $\frac{1}{3} + \frac{3}{5} = \frac{14}{15}$

29) $\frac{3}{4} - \frac{1}{2} = \frac{1}{4}$

30) $\frac{1}{2} - \frac{1}{2} = \mathbf{0}$

1) $\frac{1}{2} - \frac{2}{5} = \frac{1}{10}$

2) $\frac{1}{2} - \frac{1}{5} = \frac{3}{10}$

3) $\frac{2}{3} + \frac{1}{2} = \frac{7}{6}$ **or** $1\frac{1}{6}$

4) $\frac{3}{4} + \frac{4}{5} = \frac{31}{20}$ **or** $1\frac{11}{20}$

5) $\frac{3}{5} - \frac{1}{4} = \frac{7}{20}$

6) $\frac{1}{2} + \frac{2}{3} = \frac{7}{6}$ **or** $1\frac{1}{6}$

7) $\frac{2}{5} + \frac{1}{2} = \frac{9}{10}$

8) $\frac{3}{4} - \frac{1}{2} = \frac{1}{4}$

9) $\frac{3}{5} - \frac{1}{5} = \frac{2}{5}$

10) $\frac{1}{2} + \frac{3}{5} = \frac{11}{10}$ **or** $1\frac{1}{10}$

11) $\frac{3}{5} - \frac{1}{2} = \frac{1}{10}$

12) $\frac{1}{4} + \frac{1}{2} = \frac{3}{4}$

13) $\frac{2}{3} + \frac{1}{3} = $ **1**

14) $\frac{1}{2} - \frac{1}{2} = $ **0**

15) $\frac{3}{4} - \frac{1}{2} = \frac{1}{4}$

16) $\frac{1}{3} + \frac{1}{2} = \frac{5}{6}$

17) $\frac{1}{3} + \frac{2}{3} = $ **1**

18) $\frac{1}{2} - \frac{2}{5} = \frac{1}{10}$

19) $\frac{1}{5} + \frac{2}{3} = \frac{13}{15}$

20) $\frac{3}{5} - \frac{1}{4} = \frac{7}{20}$

21) $\frac{2}{3} - \frac{2}{3} = $ **0**

22) $1 - \frac{3}{5} = \frac{2}{5}$

23) $\frac{2}{5} + \frac{1}{2} = \frac{9}{10}$

24) $\frac{4}{5} + \frac{1}{3} = \frac{17}{15}$ **or** $1\frac{2}{15}$

25) $\frac{1}{2} + \frac{1}{2} = $ **1**

26) $\frac{2}{3} - \frac{2}{3} = $ **0**

27) $\frac{3}{4} - \frac{1}{2} = \frac{1}{4}$

28) $\frac{4}{5} + \frac{1}{2} = \frac{13}{10}$ **or** $1\frac{3}{10}$

29) $\frac{3}{4} - \frac{3}{5} = \frac{3}{20}$

30) $\frac{2}{3} + \frac{1}{2} = \frac{7}{6}$ **or** $1\frac{1}{6}$

32/42

1) $\frac{2}{3} - \frac{1}{2} = \frac{1}{6}$

2) $\frac{2}{3} + \frac{2}{3} = \frac{4}{3}$ **or** $1\frac{1}{3}$

3) $\frac{1}{3} + \frac{3}{5} = \frac{14}{15}$

4) $\frac{2}{5} - \frac{2}{5} = $ **0**

5) $\frac{3}{4} + \frac{1}{5} = \frac{19}{20}$

6) $\frac{1}{4} + \frac{2}{3} = \frac{11}{12}$

7) $\frac{3}{4} - \frac{1}{4} = \frac{1}{2}$

8) $\frac{1}{2} - \frac{1}{2} = $ **0**

9) $\frac{2}{5} - \frac{1}{4} = \frac{3}{20}$

10) $\frac{2}{3} - \frac{1}{2} = \frac{1}{6}$

11) $\frac{4}{5} + \frac{1}{2} = \frac{13}{10}$ **or** $1\frac{3}{10}$

12) $\frac{1}{4} + \frac{1}{2} = \frac{3}{4}$

13) $\frac{1}{3} + \frac{1}{3} = \frac{2}{3}$

14) $\frac{1}{2} - \frac{1}{3} = \frac{1}{6}$

15) $\frac{1}{2} + \frac{2}{3} = \frac{7}{6}$ **or** $1\frac{1}{6}$

16) $\frac{2}{3} - \frac{1}{2} = \frac{1}{6}$

17) $\frac{1}{4} + \frac{2}{3} = \frac{11}{12}$

33/42

18) $\frac{1}{2} + \frac{1}{4} = \frac{3}{4}$

19) $\frac{2}{3} - \frac{1}{4} = \frac{5}{12}$

20) $\frac{1}{2} - \frac{1}{5} = \frac{3}{10}$

21) $\frac{3}{5} - \frac{1}{3} = \frac{4}{15}$

22) $\frac{2}{3} - \frac{2}{3} = $ **0**

23) $\frac{3}{4} + \frac{1}{2} = \frac{5}{4}$ **or** $1\frac{1}{4}$

24) $\frac{1}{3} + \frac{2}{5} = \frac{11}{15}$

25) $\frac{3}{5} + \frac{3}{4} = \frac{27}{20}$ **or** $1\frac{7}{20}$

26) $\frac{1}{2} + \frac{1}{2} = $ **1**

27) $\frac{3}{4} - \frac{2}{3} = \frac{1}{12}$

28) $\frac{1}{2} - \frac{1}{3} = \frac{1}{6}$

29) $\frac{3}{4} + \frac{1}{2} = \frac{5}{4}$ **or** $1\frac{1}{4}$

30) $\frac{2}{5} - \frac{1}{4} = \frac{3}{20}$

1) $\frac{1}{3} - \frac{1}{4} = \frac{1}{12}$

2) $\frac{1}{3} + \frac{2}{3} =$ **1**

3) $\frac{3}{4} - \frac{1}{2} = \frac{1}{4}$

4) $\frac{1}{2} + \frac{1}{2} =$ **1**

5) $\frac{4}{5} - \frac{1}{3} = \frac{7}{15}$

6) $\frac{3}{4} - \frac{2}{5} = \frac{7}{20}$

7) $\frac{4}{5} + \frac{1}{2} = \frac{13}{10}$ **or** $1\frac{3}{10}$

8) $\frac{1}{4} + \frac{1}{2} = \frac{3}{4}$

9) $\frac{3}{4} + \frac{1}{2} = \frac{5}{4}$ **or** $1\frac{1}{4}$

10) $\frac{2}{3} - \frac{1}{2} = \frac{1}{6}$

11) $\frac{1}{2} - \frac{1}{2} =$ **0**

12) $\frac{1}{4} + \frac{1}{2} = \frac{3}{4}$

13) $\frac{1}{2} + \frac{3}{5} = \frac{11}{10}$ **or** $1\frac{1}{10}$

14) $\frac{1}{2} + \frac{1}{2} =$ **1**

15) $\frac{3}{5} - \frac{1}{2} = \frac{1}{10}$

16) $\frac{1}{2} - \frac{1}{4} = \frac{1}{4}$

17) $\frac{2}{3} - \frac{2}{3} =$ **0**

18) $\frac{1}{3} + \frac{1}{4} = \frac{7}{12}$

19) $\frac{4}{5} - \frac{3}{4} = \frac{1}{20}$

20) $\frac{1}{2} + \frac{1}{2} =$ **1**

21) $\frac{3}{5} + \frac{1}{2} = \frac{11}{10}$ **or** $1\frac{1}{10}$

22) $\frac{1}{2} - \frac{1}{4} = \frac{1}{4}$

23) $\frac{2}{3} + \frac{4}{5} = \frac{22}{15}$ **or** $1\frac{7}{15}$

24) $\frac{4}{5} - \frac{1}{4} = \frac{11}{20}$

25) $\frac{1}{2} + \frac{3}{5} = \frac{11}{10}$ **or** $1\frac{1}{10}$

26) $\frac{2}{5} - \frac{1}{4} = \frac{3}{20}$

27) $\frac{2}{3} + \frac{1}{3} =$ **1**

28) $\frac{3}{4} - \frac{1}{2} = \frac{1}{4}$

29) $\frac{2}{3} - \frac{1}{2} = \frac{1}{6}$

30) $\frac{4}{5} - \frac{1}{4} = \frac{11}{20}$

34/42

1) $\frac{2}{5} + \frac{1}{2} = \frac{9}{10}$

2) $\frac{2}{3} - \frac{1}{2} = \frac{1}{6}$

3) $\frac{3}{4} - \frac{3}{5} = \frac{3}{20}$

4) $\frac{4}{5} + \frac{2}{5} = \frac{6}{5}$ **or** $1\frac{1}{5}$

5) $\frac{4}{5} - \frac{1}{2} = \frac{3}{10}$

6) $\frac{3}{5} + \frac{1}{2} = \frac{11}{10}$ **or** $1\frac{1}{10}$

7) $\frac{1}{2} + \frac{1}{4} = \frac{3}{4}$

8) $\frac{3}{4} - \frac{1}{2} = \frac{1}{4}$

9) $\frac{1}{2} - \frac{1}{5} = \frac{3}{10}$

10) $\frac{2}{5} + \frac{1}{2} = \frac{9}{10}$

11) $\frac{1}{5} + \frac{1}{2} = \frac{7}{10}$

12) $\frac{1}{3} - \frac{1}{4} = \frac{1}{12}$

13) $\frac{1}{2} + \frac{1}{2} =$ **1**

14) $\frac{3}{4} - \frac{3}{5} = \frac{3}{20}$

15) $\frac{4}{5} + \frac{1}{4} = \frac{21}{20}$ **or** $1\frac{1}{20}$

16) $1 - \frac{2}{3} = \frac{1}{3}$

17) $\frac{1}{2} + \frac{1}{4} = \frac{3}{4}$

18) $\frac{4}{5} - \frac{3}{4} = \frac{1}{20}$

19) $\frac{1}{2} + \frac{1}{3} = \frac{5}{6}$

20) $\frac{3}{4} - \frac{1}{3} = \frac{5}{12}$

21) $\frac{3}{5} - \frac{1}{2} = \frac{1}{10}$

22) $\frac{1}{3} + \frac{1}{2} = \frac{5}{6}$

23) $\frac{4}{5} - \frac{2}{5} = \frac{2}{5}$

24) $\frac{1}{5} + \frac{1}{2} = \frac{7}{10}$

25) $\frac{1}{2} + \frac{2}{3} = \frac{7}{6}$ **or** $1\frac{1}{6}$

26) $\frac{2}{3} - \frac{1}{4} = \frac{5}{12}$

27) $\frac{4}{5} + \frac{1}{2} = \frac{13}{10}$ **or** $1\frac{3}{10}$

28) $\frac{2}{3} - \frac{1}{2} = \frac{1}{6}$

29) $\frac{1}{4} + \frac{1}{2} = \frac{3}{4}$

30) $\frac{1}{2} - \frac{1}{2} =$ **0**

35/42

1) $\frac{16}{3} - \frac{9}{4} = \frac{37}{12}$ **or** $3\frac{1}{12}$

2) $\frac{5}{4} + \frac{23}{7} = \frac{127}{28}$ **or** $4\frac{15}{28}$

3) $\frac{11}{4} + \frac{1}{4} = $ **3**

4) $2 - \frac{8}{7} = \frac{6}{7}$

5) $4 + \frac{9}{2} = \frac{17}{2}$ **or** $8\frac{1}{2}$

6) $\frac{7}{2} - \frac{4}{3} = \frac{13}{6}$ **or** $2\frac{1}{6}$

7) $3 - \frac{3}{2} = \frac{3}{2}$ **or** $1\frac{1}{2}$

8) $\frac{9}{2} + \frac{34}{7} = \frac{131}{14}$ **or** $9\frac{5}{14}$

9) $\frac{3}{2} - 1 = \frac{1}{2}$

10) $\frac{7}{6} + \frac{39}{8} = \frac{145}{24}$ **or** $6\frac{1}{24}$

11) $2 - \frac{1}{4} = \frac{7}{4}$ **or** $1\frac{3}{4}$

12) $\frac{4}{3} + \frac{11}{3} = $ **5**

13) $\frac{10}{3} - \frac{7}{3} = $ **1**

14) $\frac{29}{6} - 1 = \frac{23}{6}$ **or** $3\frac{5}{6}$

15) $4 + \frac{3}{2} = \frac{11}{2}$ **or** $5\frac{1}{2}$

16) $\frac{1}{2} + \frac{25}{6} = \frac{14}{3}$ **or** $4\frac{2}{3}$

36/42

17) $5 - \frac{29}{8} = \frac{11}{8}$ **or** $1\frac{3}{8}$

18) $\frac{7}{3} + 2 = \frac{13}{3}$ **or** $4\frac{1}{3}$

19) $\frac{3}{2} + 1 = \frac{5}{2}$ **or** $2\frac{1}{2}$

20) $\frac{7}{2} - \frac{7}{3} = \frac{7}{6}$ **or** $1\frac{1}{6}$

21) $\frac{19}{4} - 4 = \frac{3}{4}$

22) $\frac{31}{8} + \frac{25}{8} = $ **7**

23) $\frac{5}{2} + 3 = \frac{11}{2}$ **or** $5\frac{1}{2}$

24) $4 - \frac{2}{3} = \frac{10}{3}$ **or** $3\frac{1}{3}$

25) $\frac{16}{5} + 1 = \frac{21}{5}$ **or** $4\frac{1}{5}$

26) $\frac{19}{4} - 4 = \frac{3}{4}$

27) $\frac{5}{2} - \frac{13}{7} = \frac{9}{14}$

28) $\frac{7}{2} + \frac{7}{2} = $ **7**

29) $\frac{13}{3} - \frac{9}{8} = \frac{77}{24}$ **or** $3\frac{5}{24}$

30) $\frac{17}{6} + \frac{25}{6} = $ **7**

1) $\frac{13}{8} + \frac{9}{2} = \frac{49}{8}$ **or** $6\frac{1}{8}$

2) $\frac{10}{3} + \frac{21}{5} = \frac{113}{15}$ **or** $7\frac{8}{15}$

3) $\frac{5}{2} - 2 = \frac{1}{2}$

4) $\frac{31}{7} - \frac{2}{7} = \frac{29}{7}$ **or** $4\frac{1}{7}$

5) $\frac{29}{6} - 3 = \frac{11}{6}$ **or** $1\frac{5}{6}$

6) $\frac{27}{7} - \frac{5}{2} = \frac{19}{14}$ **or** $1\frac{5}{14}$

7) $\frac{7}{6} + \frac{24}{5} = \frac{179}{30}$ **or** $5\frac{29}{30}$

8) $\frac{15}{4} + \frac{10}{3} = \frac{85}{12}$ **or** $7\frac{1}{12}$

9) $\frac{13}{5} - \frac{5}{3} = \frac{14}{15}$

10) $\frac{9}{7} + \frac{15}{8} = \frac{177}{56}$ **or** $3\frac{9}{56}$

11) $\frac{22}{5} - 2 = \frac{12}{5}$ **or** $2\frac{2}{5}$

12) $\frac{16}{7} + 1 = \frac{23}{7}$ **or** $3\frac{2}{7}$

13) $\frac{4}{5} + 3 = \frac{19}{5}$ **or** $3\frac{4}{5}$

14) $1 + \frac{17}{4} = \frac{21}{4}$ **or** $5\frac{1}{4}$

15) $\frac{7}{2} - \frac{1}{7} = \frac{47}{14}$ **or** $3\frac{5}{14}$

16) $5 - \frac{1}{3} = \frac{14}{3}$ **or** $4\frac{2}{3}$

17) $\frac{2}{3} + \frac{13}{3} = $ **5**

18) $\frac{8}{7} - 1 = \frac{1}{7}$

19) $4 + \frac{31}{6} = \frac{55}{6}$ **or** $9\frac{1}{6}$

20) $\frac{29}{8} - \frac{11}{4} = \frac{7}{8}$

21) $4 - \frac{5}{7} = \frac{23}{7}$ **or** $3\frac{2}{7}$

22) $2 + \frac{18}{7} = \frac{32}{7}$ **or** $4\frac{4}{7}$

23) $\frac{7}{2} - \frac{3}{4} = \frac{11}{4}$ **or** $2\frac{3}{4}$

24) $\frac{4}{3} + \frac{7}{4} = \frac{37}{12}$ **or** $3\frac{1}{12}$

25) $\frac{21}{4} - \frac{7}{6} = \frac{49}{12}$ **or** $4\frac{1}{12}$

26) $\frac{14}{3} - \frac{11}{8} = \frac{79}{24}$ **or** $3\frac{7}{24}$

27) $\frac{9}{4} + \frac{3}{2} = \frac{15}{4}$ **or** $3\frac{3}{4}$

28) $\frac{26}{7} + \frac{13}{3} = \frac{169}{21}$ **or** $8\frac{1}{21}$

29) $\frac{11}{5} + 2 = \frac{21}{5}$ **or** $4\frac{1}{5}$

30) $\frac{13}{4} - \frac{3}{2} = \frac{7}{4}$ **or** $1\frac{3}{4}$

37/42

1) $\frac{8}{3} - \frac{2}{5} = \frac{34}{15}$ **or** $2\frac{4}{15}$

2) $\frac{8}{7} + 5 = \frac{43}{7}$ **or** $6\frac{1}{7}$

3) $\frac{11}{2} - 3 = \frac{5}{2}$ **or** $2\frac{1}{2}$

4) $\frac{11}{7} + \frac{13}{5} = \frac{146}{35}$ **or** $4\frac{6}{35}$

5) $5 - \frac{11}{8} = \frac{29}{8}$ **or** $3\frac{5}{8}$

6) $\frac{24}{5} - \frac{2}{7} = \frac{158}{35}$ **or** $4\frac{18}{35}$

7) $\frac{7}{2} + 3 = \frac{13}{2}$ **or** $6\frac{1}{2}$

8) $\frac{13}{3} + 5 = \frac{28}{3}$ **or** $9\frac{1}{3}$

9) $\frac{2}{7} + 4 = \frac{30}{7}$ **or** $4\frac{2}{7}$

10) $\frac{5}{8} - \frac{2}{5} = \frac{9}{40}$

11) $\frac{3}{4} - \frac{2}{3} = \frac{1}{12}$

12) $\frac{5}{2} + \frac{4}{3} = \frac{23}{6}$ **or** $3\frac{5}{6}$

13) $\frac{29}{8} - \frac{11}{7} = \frac{115}{56}$ **or** $2\frac{3}{56}$

14) $\frac{4}{3} + \frac{5}{2} = \frac{23}{6}$ **or** $3\frac{5}{6}$

15) $\frac{6}{7} + \frac{14}{3} = \frac{116}{21}$ **or** $5\frac{11}{21}$

16) $\frac{7}{2} - \frac{8}{3} = \frac{5}{6}$

17) $\frac{9}{2} - \frac{4}{7} = \frac{55}{14}$ **or** $3\frac{13}{14}$

38/42

18) $\frac{3}{2} + \frac{1}{2} = $ **2**

19) $\frac{5}{2} + \frac{2}{3} = \frac{19}{6}$ **or** $3\frac{1}{6}$

20) $4 - \frac{18}{5} = \frac{2}{5}$

21) $\frac{3}{2} - \frac{2}{3} = \frac{5}{6}$

22) $\frac{25}{8} + \frac{5}{4} = \frac{35}{8}$ **or** $4\frac{3}{8}$

23) $\frac{7}{3} - \frac{5}{6} = \frac{3}{2}$ **or** $1\frac{1}{2}$

24) $1 + \frac{9}{2} = \frac{11}{2}$ **or** $5\frac{1}{2}$

25) $\frac{33}{8} + \frac{8}{7} = \frac{295}{56}$ **or** $5\frac{15}{56}$

26) $\frac{19}{6} - \frac{3}{8} = \frac{67}{24}$ **or** $2\frac{19}{24}$

27) $\frac{25}{8} - \frac{5}{3} = \frac{35}{24}$ **or** $1\frac{11}{24}$

28) $\frac{25}{7} + \frac{11}{3} = \frac{152}{21}$ **or** $7\frac{5}{21}$

29) $\frac{26}{7} + \frac{9}{2} = \frac{115}{14}$ **or** $8\frac{3}{14}$

30) $\frac{13}{3} - 2 = \frac{7}{3}$ **or** $2\frac{1}{3}$

1) $\frac{1}{3} + \frac{11}{4} = \frac{37}{12}$ **or** $3\frac{1}{12}$

2) $\frac{1}{2} + \frac{4}{3} = \frac{11}{6}$ **or** $1\frac{5}{6}$

3) $\frac{14}{3} - 4 = \frac{2}{3}$

4) $\frac{19}{5} - \frac{5}{2} = \frac{13}{10}$ **or** $1\frac{3}{10}$

5) $\frac{5}{8} + \frac{3}{4} = \frac{11}{8}$ **or** $1\frac{3}{8}$

6) $5 + \frac{1}{4} = \frac{21}{4}$ **or** $5\frac{1}{4}$

7) $\frac{23}{6} - 1 = \frac{17}{6}$ **or** $2\frac{5}{6}$

8) $\frac{29}{6} - \frac{9}{2} = \frac{1}{3}$

9) $\frac{9}{2} - \frac{12}{5} = \frac{21}{10}$ **or** $2\frac{1}{10}$

10) $3 - \frac{11}{6} = \frac{7}{6}$ **or** $1\frac{1}{6}$

11) $\frac{13}{4} + \frac{5}{4} = \frac{9}{2}$ **or** $4\frac{1}{2}$

12) $\frac{2}{7} + 4 = \frac{30}{7}$ **or** $4\frac{2}{7}$

13) $\frac{23}{6} - \frac{25}{7} = \frac{11}{42}$

14) $\frac{7}{2} - \frac{1}{6} = \frac{10}{3}$ **or** $3\frac{1}{3}$

15) $\frac{10}{3} + 1 = \frac{13}{3}$ **or** $4\frac{1}{3}$

16) $\frac{8}{3} + \frac{31}{8} = \frac{157}{24}$ **or** $6\frac{13}{24}$

17) $\frac{22}{5} + \frac{17}{4} = \frac{173}{20}$ **or** $8\frac{13}{20}$

39/42

18) $\frac{2}{3} + \frac{3}{2} = \frac{13}{6}$ **or** $2\frac{1}{6}$

19) $\frac{17}{5} - \frac{1}{2} = \frac{29}{10}$ **or** $2\frac{9}{10}$

20) $\frac{33}{7} - \frac{14}{3} = \frac{1}{21}$

21) $4 + \frac{31}{7} = \frac{59}{7}$ **or** $8\frac{3}{7}$

22) $\frac{5}{2} - \frac{2}{5} = \frac{21}{10}$ **or** $2\frac{1}{10}$

23) $\frac{5}{2} + \frac{9}{2} = $ **7**

24) $\frac{19}{4} - \frac{19}{6} = \frac{19}{12}$ **or** $1\frac{7}{12}$

25) $\frac{25}{8} - 3 = \frac{1}{8}$

26) $4 + \frac{5}{6} = \frac{29}{6}$ **or** $4\frac{5}{6}$

27) $3 + \frac{13}{5} = \frac{28}{5}$ **or** $5\frac{3}{5}$

28) $\frac{9}{2} - \frac{8}{5} = \frac{29}{10}$ **or** $2\frac{9}{10}$

29) $1 + \frac{13}{4} = \frac{17}{4}$ **or** $4\frac{1}{4}$

30) $3 - \frac{3}{2} = \frac{3}{2}$ **or** $1\frac{1}{2}$

1) $\frac{11}{5} + \frac{7}{4} = \frac{79}{20}$ **or** $3\frac{19}{20}$

2) $\frac{10}{7} + \frac{22}{7} = \frac{32}{7}$ **or** $4\frac{4}{7}$

3) $\frac{14}{3} - 2 = \frac{8}{3}$ **or** $2\frac{2}{3}$

4) $4 - \frac{3}{2} = \frac{5}{2}$ **or** $2\frac{1}{2}$

5) $\frac{13}{3} - \frac{8}{3} = \frac{5}{3}$ **or** $1\frac{2}{3}$

6) $2 + \frac{7}{2} = \frac{11}{2}$ **or** $5\frac{1}{2}$

7) $\frac{5}{2} - \frac{11}{5} = \frac{3}{10}$

8) $\frac{9}{5} + \frac{9}{2} = \frac{63}{10}$ **or** $6\frac{3}{10}$

9) $\frac{1}{2} + \frac{5}{4} = \frac{7}{4}$ **or** $1\frac{3}{4}$

10) $1 + \frac{13}{4} = \frac{17}{4}$ **or** $4\frac{1}{4}$

11) $5 - \frac{20}{7} = \frac{15}{7}$ **or** $2\frac{1}{7}$

12) $\frac{15}{4} - \frac{1}{4} = \frac{7}{2}$ **or** $3\frac{1}{2}$

13) $\frac{7}{2} - \frac{8}{5} = \frac{19}{10}$ **or** $1\frac{9}{10}$

14) $\frac{9}{2} - \frac{31}{8} = \frac{5}{8}$

15) $\frac{16}{5} + \frac{22}{7} = \frac{222}{35}$ **or** $6\frac{12}{35}$

16) $\frac{14}{3} + \frac{5}{2} = \frac{43}{6}$ **or** $7\frac{1}{6}$

40/42

17) $\frac{2}{5} + \frac{29}{6} = \frac{157}{30}$ **or** $5\frac{7}{30}$

18) $3 - \frac{13}{5} = \frac{2}{5}$

19) $\frac{21}{5} + \frac{19}{6} = \frac{221}{30}$ **or** $7\frac{11}{30}$

20) $\frac{7}{3} - \frac{2}{3} = \frac{5}{3}$ **or** $1\frac{2}{3}$

21) $\frac{3}{2} + \frac{15}{4} = \frac{21}{4}$ **or** $5\frac{1}{4}$

22) $\frac{3}{2} - \frac{1}{7} = \frac{19}{14}$ **or** $1\frac{5}{14}$

23) $1 + \frac{3}{5} = \frac{8}{5}$ **or** $1\frac{3}{5}$

24) $\frac{9}{2} - 4 = \frac{1}{2}$

25) $3 + \frac{1}{4} = \frac{13}{4}$ **or** $3\frac{1}{4}$

26) $\frac{5}{3} + \frac{13}{4} = \frac{59}{12}$ **or** $4\frac{11}{12}$

27) $\frac{1}{3} - \frac{1}{3} = \mathbf{0}$

28) $\frac{16}{3} - \frac{9}{2} = \frac{5}{6}$

29) $\frac{23}{5} + \frac{14}{3} = \frac{139}{15}$ **or** $9\frac{4}{15}$

30) $\frac{18}{7} - 1 = \frac{11}{7}$ **or** $1\frac{4}{7}$